The Big Book
of Knives

The Big Book of Knives

Everything about Mankind's Most Important Tool

Oliver Lang

SCHIFFER
PUBLISHING

4880 Lower Valley Road • Atglen, PA 19310

Edited by Ian Robertson
Cover design by Justin Watkinson
Type set in Gotham

Contents

Foreword

Although it is mid-March and early in the morning, the sun's rays are already warming. I know this so precisely because I have just arrived at the computer screen. Before that, I was outside grinding a new point on a broken knife blade—the first strokes to smooth the broken edge on the natural stone of the terrace surface, the rest on a coarse stone, and finally sandpaper. As a result, the formerly typical Mediterranean blade shape, resembling a saber blade, became a somewhat shorter Catalonian *santoku* blade.

The knife came from Pallarès Solsona of Spain. It had previously lost its tip during careless handling. After that, the carbon-steel knife saw service as a package opener and test knife. (You can see its battered blade on page 183 of this book, where it is used to demonstrate sharpening on river stones.) New, this knife would cost just twelve dollars.

Why the trouble then? Because the work and the expertise that David—the owner of Pallarès Solsona—invested in the making of the knife makes it worthwhile. And I like it—it reminds me of the *capuchadou*, the fixed knife used daily by the French agricultural workers of the nineteenth century—because it is a handy, good knife just as good for a picnic as it is for cutting rope, or sharpening a stick, and also because reworking the knife was fun.

If you are moved by these same personal motives, then this book is for you. If you wish to discover the exciting world hidden behind such a seemingly simple tool as the knife, then here you will find what you are seeking. Here you will learn why knives look the way they do, and how knives are made and forged, cared for, and sharpened.

Incidentally, one of the knives on the back of the book is the first knife I can consciously remember. It belonged to my father and his older brother, both of whom were born in the 1930s. Previously it had been in a blue metal tool box and was inaccessible to me.

The knife and the tool box have been with me for a long time now and are even included in this book. While my father regularly confiscated my sharp new acquisitions in my younger years, he nevertheless inspired me when every evening he wielded a bread knife, cutting absolutely identical slices of bread freehand.

This book would not have come about without the help of many people. Thanks are due to all the knife makers and forgers who invited me to have a firsthand look at their work practices, especially Heiner Schmidbauer and Tobias Haselmayr. I would also like to thank the passionate knife makers who put me in touch with the history of the knife and their knives. In particular, I would like to name Giselheid Herder-Scholz (Herder), Sal and Eric Glesser (Spyderco), Wolfgang Lantelme (Passion France), Henning Ritter (Hubertus), and Stefan Rosenkaimer (Lindner). My heartfelt thanks also go to all knife makers and dealers for sending test knives and photos, and to Mark Christensen of Blade HQ. Not least I wish to thank Ulrich Gerfin and Roman Landes, who freely share their valuable knowledge about steels and blades in Knife Forum and in books, as well as my editor for his trust, Karola Wieland for his encouragement and final editing, Dr. Stefan Schmalhaus and Dr. Can Dörtbudak for editing, and in particular Caroline Wydeau, who arranged this book with patience and feeling.

Behind every good knife is an idea, a history, a world of physics and chemistry, craftsmanship, and art. The journey of discovery begins.

Oliver Lang
Übersee, March 2017

A simple knife but a piece with ideal value: the author put the broken blade of this Spanish Pallarès Solsona back in working order, using the simplest means.

Chapter 1. Introduction

Knife Fascination

Hand tools for cutting are among humanity's oldest equipment. To many anthropologists and cultural scientists they are also the most important.

If one looks to the beginning of early humans, one recognizes the full extent of the knife's importance: the first sharp-edged, knapped flint stones changed the ability of humans to procure food, as well as their eating habits, and thus also influenced the formation of human communities. It was not until the advent of the knife and its sharp descendents—the ax and the saw—that it became possible for humans to create other tools, giving them security and promoting their further development.

Is this perhaps the reason why so many of us in our modern, highly modernized world have such interest, respect, and appreciation for an archaic—and probably simple—tool such as the knife? Is the desire for the perfect knife in our genes?

That is possible, but despite the desire for a good knife, despite the long shared history, and despite its practical use, many people no longer know what makes a good knife and how to recognize one, how to handle it, how to use it safely and effectively, and how to care for and sharpen it.

Reading this book will change that. Let yourself become infected with "knife fascination." Dive into the exciting knife cosmos, which will lead you from A, as in ABS, to Z, as in Zytel (both are plastics used for making knife handles). Become a passionate knife expert and learn everything one should know about knives.

This is worthwhile, since once one has found one's perfect knife, one will not want to do without it. But be warned; experience

In the "cottage" typical of the Solingen knife industry, the large grindstones were driven by waterpower.

11

The first sharp-edged flint tools radically changed humans' capabilities and living conditions.

Copper tools were a major advance. Ötzi (the nickname given to a well-preserved natural mummy of a man who lived and died between 3359 and 3105 BCE, found in the Ötztal Alps), carried a copper axe. Photo: *South Tyrol Archaeological Museum, www.iceman.it*

has shown that if one believes that one has finally found the ideal knife, a new temptation always appears. The world of knives is simply too fascinating and wide ranging. There is much to discover.

The History of the Knife

The first specially shaped stone tools appeared about 3.4 million years ago. And so it remained for a very long time. The decisive change did not come about until the discovery of metal extraction about 7,000 years ago. The use of copper, followed by bronze and, another 1,500 years later, iron was among the most-important steps in human history toward the modern world that we know today.

Bronze could be formed into weapons, tools, and jewelry. The metal was expensive and led to the establishment of trade relations over thousands of miles. One of the special things about bronze is that it is an alloy that does not occur in nature.

What led men to heat seemingly ordinary stone to the point that copper and tin were rendered? What led them to combine these two metals in a certain ratio to make bronze, which was much harder than either? It borders on a miracle.

Even more miraculous is the utilization of iron. It is true that the earth's core consists largely of iron and that iron ore can be found on the surface in many places, but extracting the iron from rock is extremely difficult.

In central Europe, people first succeeded in doing this in the eighth century. This was made possible by highly efficient furnaces in which iron ore could be heated with the help of wood charcoal to temperatures high enough to produce so-called iron puddle balls. These were spongy, carbonaceous lumps of iron from which an expert smith could produce high-grade steel. Such a versatile and high-grade material had never before existed. Until the thirteenth century, such bloomery furnaces were the only way of producing steel.

From the thirteenth century onward, the major centers for knife production developed where there were sources of iron ore combined with usable waterpower, supplies of wood, and the necessary knowledge. The major centers in Europe were Solingen (Germany); Chatellerault,

Iron ore was smelted in so-called bloomery furnaces. Left behind was a slag-filled iron puddle ball.

The English-language *German Knife and Sword Makers* is the standard work on knife making between 1850 and 1945.

For centuries, Solingen was one of the world's most important manufacturing centers for knives and other cutlery. Illustration from the book *German Knife and Sword Makers*.

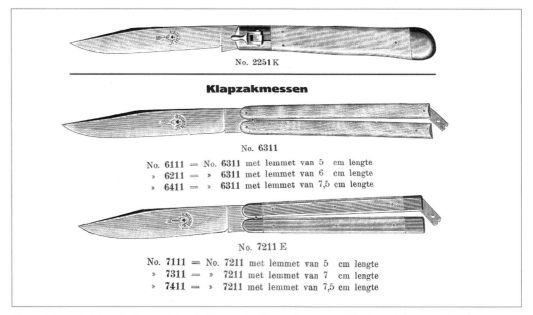

The old model books issued by Solingen knife makers are filled with interesting but in some cases long-forgotten knife types. The traditional "butterfly knife" is no longer permitted.

Nogent, Nontron, Paris, and Thiers (France); Sheffield and London (England); Scarperia and Maniago (Italy); Toledo (Spain); and Eskilstuna and Mora (Sweden). For centuries, there have also been traditional and highly specialized centers such as Seki, in Japan. With European emigration from England and Germany, more than 200 years ago the art of knife making also reached the United States, which today is one of the most important knife-producing countries, providing the world market with sharp blades alongside China.

Solingen—Germany's Blade City

Located in North Rhine–Westphalia, Solingen is the undisputed center of German cutlery. The city at the edge of the Bergisches Land region is so well known around the world for knives and scissors that Solingen is sometimes mistaken for a brand of knife. It is for good reason that since 2012, the title "Blade City" has officially been added to the city's name.

Blade weapons were produced in Solingen as early as the thirteenth century. After Solingen was granted civic rights in 1371, the dictum *Me fecit Solingen* (Solingen Made Me) adorned countless blades. In the beginning, this was especially true of swords. Solingen's pride in this tradition is reflected in its street names: Sword Street, Dagger Street, Foil Way, Blade Street, Knife Street, etc.

All the resources needed for forging and grinding blades are present in the country around Solingen: iron ore deposits, forests with large stands of oak to fire low-carbon steel, and numerous streams and the Wupper River, which powered forging hammers and grinding stones and whose cold water quenched and thus hardened the forged blade steel.

Among Solingen's greatest resources was its resident expertise: its artisans were strongly organized in brotherhoods. By the beginning of the fifteenth century there were already guilds of grinders and hardeners, sword makers, and swordsmiths. With hammer and anvil, the swordsmith shaped steel into sword, dagger, or saber form. The hardener turned these blanks into hard blades through controlled heating and abrupt quenching. Then they went to the

Since 2012, Solingen has officially been called Blade City. At the beginning of the fifteenth century there were guilds for swordsmiths and grinders in the city.

grinder. These grinders either worked their own cottages or rented rooms in larger houses. They housed the disc-shaped grinding stones that gave the blades their ultimate form and sharpness.

Finally, it was the sword makers who smoothed and polished the blades to refine the preceding steps. They assembled the individual parts and combined the handle and blade into a whole. It was also the sword makers who marketed the edged weapons. Since their skills were not as substantial as those of the other guilds—in contrast to all the other blade craftsmen—they also had to travel.

The travel and work ban for smiths, grinders, and hardeners was intended to prevent the expertise from leaving and damaging the city of Solingen. By the mid-1700s at the latest, more and more specialized workers from Solingen set up shop in other German cities or immigrated to France, Sweden, England, Russia, and America.

The sword-making craft is also so significant because the other craftsmanships developed from it. The knife maker's guild is mentioned for the first time in 1571. A good 200 years later (1794) the scissors makers combined to form a new guild.

Solingen is still a sought-after European knife-making center. The knife makers

Swiss knife maker Victorinox depicts the evolution of the knife as follows: from a Stone Age hand ax to a multifunction everyday tool.

guild is history, however, and the trade of knifesmith no longer exists in this form: today they are cutting-tool mechanics, so to speak. In fact, this term is technically correct and more precise than that of blacksmith, because for the most part there is no longer any smithing done. Industrially, one works with modern machines such as laser cutters and CSC milling automatons. (To learn how a simple piece of steel becomes a knife, read chapter 10.)

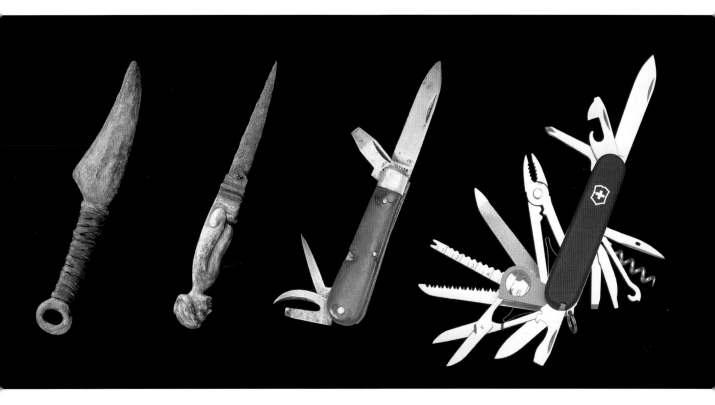

Chapter Summary

Sharp-edged pieces of flint were humanity's first knives. At first they were probably found that way, but later they were precisely and expertly shaped. Their use changed the lives and communities of early humans forever. The knife is humanity's oldest and most important tool.

The first metal was smelted about 7,000 years ago, and blades were made from it. Copper was followed by harder bronze alloy. Almost 3,000 years ago, humans first succeeded in obtaining and using iron. It was this important development that made our modern world possible.

The major knife-producing centers such as Sheffield in England and Solingen in Germany developed from the thirteenth century onward. Since 2012, Solingen has officially born the title "Blade City."

Chapter 2.
Fixed Knives:
Trusty Companions

Knives whose blade and grip form a single unit are called fixed knives. Their opposite numbers are folding knives, whose blade can be folded into the handle. For a long time the fixed-blade knife was humanity's most important cutting instrument, until the folding knife began its triumphant march in the early nineteenth century.

Despite this, the popularity of fixed knives continues to this day. It is the first choice wherever one must rely to a special degree on one's knife and where carrying comfort or concealed carriage is not a priority. As a rule, a fixed-blade knife is more durable than a folding knife, with its many parts. A fixed-blade knife has no lock that can fail and possibly endanger the user. And once it is pulled from its sheath, the knife is immediately usable and does not have to be unfolded.

The designers of a fixed-blade knife have more possibilities, since they do not have to take into account the mechanical design features of a folding knife. As a rule, fixed-blade knives are also easier to clean. They are therefore especially well suited to certain uses, such as hunting or outdoor knives, military knives, and divers' knives.

Construction Methods

The relevant criterion for distinguishing between various fixed-blade knives is the design of the tang and handle. Here you will learn about the full tang and hidden tang, and fully and half-integral knives.

Flat-Tang Knives

On a flat-tang knife, the blade and tang have the same—or almost the same—width and height, and the tang extends to the handle end. If the tang retains its initial height it is called a full tang. The tang's height can decrease toward the handle end, which leads to a front-heavy weight distribution. The total weight is also reduced without significantly affecting the knife's stability. The flat-tang construction method is considered very sturdy.

Flat-tang knives usually have a handle consisting of two scales with the tang sandwiched between them. These can be made of wood, horn, or other material (more on this in chapter 8) and, as a rule,

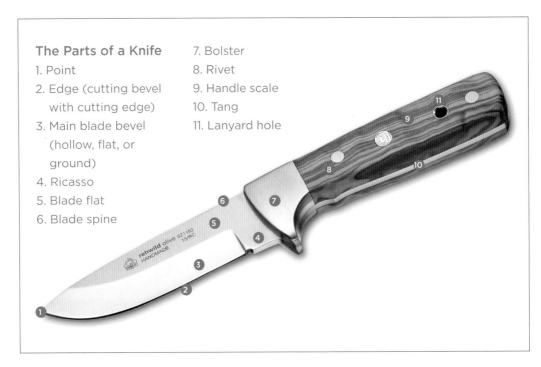

The Parts of a Knife
1. Point
2. Edge (cutting bevel with cutting edge)
3. Main blade bevel (hollow, flat, or ground)
4. Ricasso
5. Blade flat
6. Blade spine
7. Bolster
8. Rivet
9. Handle scale
10. Tang
11. Lanyard hole

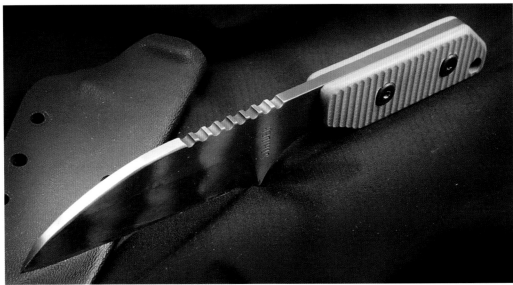

The flat-tang design of this sturdy operational knife by Strider (JS model) is clearly visible: the blade thickness is retained by the tang all the way to the end of the handle.

If the handle bolsters are an integral part of the blade—not superimposed—then it must be a half-integral knife. *Messer-Werk.de*

On a fully integral knife, the blade, as well as the front and rear bolsters, is made from one and the same piece of steel. *Böker*

are attached to the tang with rivet pins or screws and are often also glued. There are also full-steel knives (without handle scales) and variants with a wound handle of cord.

Half-Integral and Fully Integral Knives

On a half-integral knife, the bolsters are not mounted; instead, they are made from the same piece of steel as the blade. A fully integral knife also has a bolster or pommel at the end of the handle, which is also formed from the same piece and is thus an integral part of the design.

Half- and fully integral knives can be milled from a solid piece of steel, which is an expensive procedure. For larger numbers, production in a drop forge makes more sense. The steel blank is heated until red hot and placed in the so-called bottom die. The counterpart to this is the ram. The later

On hidden-tang knives, the blade turns into a tapering tang, which is later fully enclosed by the handle. Seen here is a blank of Damast steel by Ulrich Gerfin.

shape of the knife is placed in these two dies as a negative template. To shape the blank into the knife, an extremely heavy drop hammer—which is called the bear and carries the ram—is dropped onto the blank in the bottom die. The impact forces are extremely high (as is the noise), and these reshape the steel.

Half- and fully integral knives are considered very strong. Because of their massive bolsters the knives are relatively heavy, and the balance point is usually in the area of the handle.

Hidden-Tang Knives

On a hidden-tang knife, the blade turns into a tang that is significantly narrower and usually tapers slightly conically. It can be round or have a square profile. The tang is hidden in the handle and is enclosed by it. Typical representatives of this class are traditional Japanese cooking knives and the Nordic outdoor knife, which has been produced in Sweden, Norway, and Finland for centuries. Most hunting and combat knives by the legendary American company Randall Made Knives are made this way.

The tang often extends just a couple of inches into the handle and is glued there. In earlier days, birch tar was used, but today there is high-strength epoxy resin for this purpose. If the tang extends to the handle end, it can be compressed with aimed hammer blows and thus attached to the handle.

In other hidden-tang designs, threads are cut into the tang so that a butt plate can be screwed onto it. The threaded section can also be welded or soldered onto a short, hidden tang. Modern hidden-tang knives with thermoplastic handles have them injection-molded directly onto the tang.

A hidden-tang design makes a knife light and, if professionally made, strong enough for all cutting tasks one encounters while outdoors or hunting; even the *leuku*—the machete-like knife of the Sami (the indigenous people of northern Scandinavia)—are made this way.

The hidden-tang construction method has other advantages: the hand does not come into contact with cold steel on the edges (unlike a flat-tang knife) and the tang itself—sealed inside the handle with glue—is well protected against corrosion.

Sheaths

A fixed knife is not complete without a good sheath. One could also say somewhat pointedly that a knife is only as good as its sheath. It ensures a good grip on the knife, protects the wearer from the blade during transport, and at the same time protects the knife against damage or loss. The sheath is thus essential for the functionality of a fixed knife. Sheaths can also be very artistic and contribute to the enjoyment of a knife.

Traditionally, sheaths are made of leather (less commonly of wood or metal). Today, synthetic materials such as nylon or Kydex are being used increasingly. A sheath can be made one piece or multipiece, and depending on the material used can be sewn, screwed, riveted, or injection-molded.

The traditional Scandinavian knives are usually carried in a leather sheath that extends to just short of the handle end—like the *leuku* knife seen here (*top*). Beneath is a sheath with handle strap.

TRIVIA: Kydex: Easy to Form

Kydex is the trade name of a thermoplastic polymer. Kydex has become a popular material for knife sheaths and pistol holsters. It is considered robust, low maintenance, malleable, and—if handled properly—dimensionally stable.

If Kydex is heated to about 300 degrees Fahrenheit, it becomes as soft as cheese slices and adapts perfectly to the contours of an object. After it is cooled, the material retains this shape. Kydex can also be sanded and polished. And if an error is made during shaping, it is not a disaster: the material only needs to be heated to the necessary temperature again, and it can be reformed without having to worry about problems. All of this makes Kydex a popular material for hobbyist knife makers.

When soft materials such as leather or nylon are used, a sheath often has a plastic insert or a tough leather (called Keder) interlayer that prevents piercing and cutting along the seam.

Nordic Sheath

Sleeve sheaths enclose the knife so deeply that often only a couple of inches of the handle show. This type of sheath is typical of Nordic knives. Its custom fit and large covered area create a great deal of friction between the sheath and knife, and thus retention force. Additional security in the form of a handle strap is normally not necessary.

Sheath with Handle Strap

Sheaths that accommodate only the blade are relatively common. Even if the fit is good, another aid is needed to secure the knife.

This is usually accomplished with a strap that goes around the handle and is closable by means of a Velcro fastener or press stud. For knives with a cross guard, the strap is installed so that it passes diagonally over the guard.

Pancake Sheath

The pancake sheath resembles many pistol holsters: the two integrated belt loops beside the knife are typical features of the pancake sheath. They are often installed so that the sheath sits on the belt angled slightly, which makes it easier to grasp the knife.

Alternative Carriage Methods

The knife can be worn in other ways in addition to on the belt. Favorites include in one's boot or around the neck.

On a pancake sheath the belt passes through two loops on either side of the knife. *Pohl Force*

Boot Knife

A handy Derringer pistol or a knife hidden in a boot that could easily be reached even when sitting seems to have been part of the basic equipment for every Wild West poker game. Even today, boot knives are still made by established knife makers.

Access to a boot knife is limited by an overlapping pant leg while standing, but when kneeling, sitting, or lying down—when perhaps something has already gone wrong—a boot knife is possibly easier to reach than one on a belt. At the same time, the knife is out of the other's view and reach. Typically, boot knives have a clip sheath that can be attached to the side of the bootleg. If the sheath has eyelets, the boot laces can also be run through them. It is important that the sheath's retaining force is great enough to hold the knife securely even in a fall, and that it not hamper the wearer's mobility while walking.

Neck Knives

Neck knives are fixed knives worn around the neck, usually with the handle facing down. Compact knives are the rule, and sheaths with great retaining force are a must. To reduce the danger of strangulation, the knife is worn on a chain with a break point instead of on a cord.

Wearing a knife around one's neck makes it possible to reach it when normally worn knives are difficult to reach; for example, because a long jacket or climbing harness is in the way. Neck knives are also popular as easily reachable second knives for small, everyday tasks.

The Most-Important Classes of Knives

There are many types of knives that have developed for special uses. Here you will learn the most-important classes of knife,

Neck knife with additional security on the sheath: the Always Ready by Spyderco. *Spyderco*

The Eickhorn SEK II Boot Knife can be attached to boots with its leather clip sheath.

Knives from Helle, CRKT, Stefan Richle, and Morakniv (*from left*) that can be used as neck knives.

Nicker knives are traditional hunting knives for administering the coup de grace. Typically the blade tapers toward the tip, resulting in an almost triangular blade shape. The tang can be made as a flat or hidden tang.

Hunting knives vary from functional utility knives to elegant collector pieces. Seen here is a particularly beautiful, handmade hidden-tang hunting knife by German knife maker and hunter Heiner Schmidbauer. The blade is made of rustproof Damast steel, the handle of sambar deer horn.

their development histories, and the most important representatives.

Hunting Knife

In the wild, hunters are confronted with a wide range of tasks, from sharpening a stick for a salt lick to cutting open and gutting game. To keep the flesh of an animal hygienic, the organs and intestines must be removed as quickly as possible. This enables the body to cool much more quickly.

It is often said that "The more experienced the hunter, the shorter the blade." This may be true for the task of cutting open and gutting an animal. Another of the hunter's tasks can include giving the coup de grace to a wounded animal when a firearm cannot be used. A certain blade length is required, in this case 4.3 inches.

The *Knicker* is the traditional (German) hunting knife, and its use is widespread. It got its name because its sharp blade can be used to stab ("*abnicken*") through the cervical vertebrae of a deer, severing the spinal cord. A Knicker's easy-to-handle blade is also well suited to cutting an animal open and gutting.

Knickers come in a wide variety of construction styles: as hidden-tang, flat-tang, and even half- and fully integral knives. A one-sided guard is typical, preventing the hand from slipping toward the cutting edge.

Among those hunting knives that are historic, but scarcely still relevant, is the *Waidblatt*, a large slashing and self-defense knife. *Saufänger* (sow catchers) are long, sturdy knives that can be attached to long poles, for catching wild boar.

Outdoor Knives

In the outdoors, a dependable knife is one of man's most important tools. With it one can prepare food; clean fish; cut rope and other materials; cut timber, tent pegs, digging sticks, and other tools; split firewood; and make feathersticks for starting fires.

TRIVIA: The Nicker: Hunting Knife, Cutlery Knife, and Weapon

In *Messer und Besteck in der Lederhose*, authors Alfred Stadlbauer and Heinz Huther quote Aventinus (1477–1534), who in his *Bavarian Chronicle* wrote of the "common" Bavarian folk that they "sit drinking wine day and night, singing, dancing, playing cards and may carry defensive weapons, hog pikes and long knives." The publication repeatedly states that the long knives were "pointed knives with long blades fixed in the handles" that "were usually worn as cutlery knives in an open side pocket of the trousers." They were thus Nicker knives, carried as "all-purpose tools and as weapons just in case."

Scandinavian knives such as this classic by Morakniv are very well suited for whittling.

The handles of Nordic knives are traditionally made of native types of wood or birch bark, as here on the Finnish *Iisakki Järvenpää* (*bottom*).

There is no perfect knife, no panacea for all these tasks. This question is the topic of many discussions. But a look to Scandinavia provides inspiration. The northern countries have a long-knife culture that has lasted until the present day. Thanks to the worldwide bushcraft boom and well-known users of Swedish knives such as TV personalities Ray Mears and Cody Lundin, Scandinavian knives are today more popular than ever before.

While there are regional differences, the traditional knives of the Swedes, Norwegians, and Finns are similar in many respects. The blade is relatively narrow. The spine runs almost straight, with the edge curving up to meet the back at the tip. Over a certain part of the height—often up to two-thirds—the blade retains its full thickness, then narrows to the cutting edge without further beveling.

TRIVIA: Scandinavian Grind: Simply Sharp

The Scandinavian grind (often abbreviated as Skandi) is a wide, flat bevel that runs to the edge of a blade. There is little or no secondary bevel. To sharpen a knife with this geometry, one places it on the sharpening stone with its sides lying flat on the stone.

This method is very simple, but it is not quick, since material must be removed from the entire bevel and length. To simplify the work while on the move, the blade can also be sharpened somewhat more obtusely. This makes the cutting edge stronger. At home it can be returned to a finer angle.

With the acute-angle cutting edges the Scandinavian grind produces, one can cut extraordinarily well. One needs a steel that can bear such a small angle: non-rustproof steel, fine-grained tool steel, or moderately alloyed rustproof steel are preferred.

Because blade thickness from the cutting edge increases rapidly, as a rule Scandinavian knives are very robust. Because of the high sharpening angle there are better types of knives—depending on material—for cutting deep into something.

The *kukri* is inseparable from the country people of Nepal and the Gurhka soldiers who come from there. The preferred material for making these big chopping knives is old truck springs.

KUKRI: In the Gurhka Style

A *kukri* (also called *khukri* or *khukuri*) is unmistakable: the large inwardly curved blade, widening toward the tip, and the prominent bend in the spine and cutting-edge lines are typical for the traditional cutting tool from Nepal. Some boys receive their first *kukri* at age five to learn how to handle it properly.

Traditionally, the *kukri* was used for many purposes in Nepal: to make a way along overgrown paths, to hack branches and traps and delimb small trees, to sharpen stakes, to butcher animals, to prepare food for cooking, and also to protect against attackers, whether they be animal (there are still bears, tigers, and leopards in the wilds of Nepal) or human. Because of its length and weight, the *kukri*—with the blade spine or butt forward—can also be used as a conventional blunt instrument.

The Gurhka troops that served in the Nepalese, British, and Indian military were formerly recruited from the remote mountain people of Nepal. The *kukri* is their identifying feature and is part of their standard equipment. In their hands, the typically 12-to-16-inch-long slashers became feared weapons, even though they were more frequently used as work tools.

Equally typical is the hidden-tang design: the tang is inserted in a hole in the handle. Only the end of the tang is sometimes visible; it is not glued into the handle, instead having a base plate screwed or riveted to the handle end. A guard is rarely found on the handle, and the knife always sits deeply in the sheath. Handle and sheath are typically made of regional materials.

Everything in this knife design serves a purpose: the narrow blade is versatile. The grind leads to an acutely angled, efficient blade. The continuous thickness of the upper part of the blade provides sufficient strength. The straight spine makes it possible to exert controlled pressure with the other hand. The absence of a guard makes it simpler to grasp the knife by the blade and thus guide it. This makes it possible to precisely control the knife when making fine cuts, or when working with the tip.

A special type of outdoor knife is the survival knife with wooden handle. It played a major role in the blockbuster *First Blood* (1982), in which Sylvester Stallone plays traumatized Vietnam veteran Rambo.

Its features can be seen at every suitable opportunity: a large knife with a large blade and wooden handle containing survival accessories such as fish hooks, a compass, and matches, and wrapped with a green nylon filament that can be used as fishing line. The Rambo knife was born.

A knife that caused a sensation in the early 1980s: John Rambo's survival knife. *Master Cutlery*

A large slasher from Terävä of Finland and a freshly sharpened Othello from the 1940s.

The Prepper One from German manufacturer Pohl Force is a versatile and especially durable tactical knife.

The Ontario A.S.E.K. is a military knife often used by pilots. It is designed to assist in exiting aircraft in emergencies and for subsequent survival.

Tactical Knives, Military Knives, and Self-Defense Knives

In addition to fixed-blade tactical knives, there are also fixed-blade military knives. The two classes of knives can best be differentiated as follows: a tactical knife must be able to cut webbing and rope and be just as suitable for preparing food or firewood as for violently ripping open a steel drum, or tearing down the door of a locked shelter.

During all these actions the knife must remain sharp or be able to be sharpened again by using normal means. And it must have strength reserves, neither breaking completely in two nor breaking away along the cutting edge. It must be safe to handle and be protected against loss during carriage. And it must be big and strong enough to fend off threats. A typical tactical knife is the Prepper One from German manufacturer Pohl Force.

Military knives are blade weapons that are part of the official—and occasionally also unofficial—equipment of soldiers. The required functions have changed significantly over the past 100 years. In the trenches of the First World War, troops asked for stabbing and striking weapons, which one would now call trench knives and knuckle knives (the latter has a handle whose frame was shaped like a set of brass knuckles).

Stabbing weapons were also used in the Second World War: the most famous dagger of that epoch is the F-S Dagger developed by Ewart Fairbairn and Eric Anthony Sykes, which continues to be produced in faithful detail today.

No other type of knife stands for the American military knife like the Ka-Bar USMC (United States Marine Corps). It was developed when, after the American entry into the Second World War, numerous complaints were received from army troops and marines. They were dissatisfied with the trench knifes they had been issued, the same type used in the First World War. With its brass-knuckle finger guard, the knife sat poorly in its sheath, and the thin blade broke too easily in everyday use.

The war ministry finally acknowledged the need for a new, sturdy multipurpose knife. The specification sheet that was issued for the American fighting knife of the Second World War envisaged a long, strong blade, which to reduce weight was to have a small fuller plus a pinned pommel, a steel cross guard, a stacked leather grip, and a black phosphate coating of all metal parts. The prototype was called 1219C2 and was later rechristened USMC Mark 2 Combat Knife (also known as Knife, Fighting Utility).

The knife was produced by a number of manufacturers, such as Camillus, Union Cutlery Company, and Robeson and Pal. The Union Cutlery Company was the only supplier that consistently marked its combat and all-purpose knife—with the Ka-Bar trademark (more on this in the information box on the next page). A million true Ka-Bars were produced during the war. Ka-Bar became a symbol for the military knives used by American soldiers and marines, with whose help they repaired equipment, dug trenches, cut tent pegs and dug in the earth, opened tinned food, pried open crates, and sometimes even defended their lives.

In the present day, military knives have been designed as multipurpose cutting and chopping tools, which are used and also misused for rescue operations, constructing shelters, modifying equipment, camp work, preparing food, and everything that comes to mind. A military knife must be able to stand up to being used to pry open a crate or as a can opener and then being stuck in its sheath without being cleaned.

A good example of such a knife is the A.S.E.K. (Aircraft Survival Egress Knife) from the American Ontario Knife Company. The survival and egress knife was developed for crewmen of US Air Force aircraft such as the Blackhawk helicopter.

A knife is designated tactical if it was developed specifically or is suitable for defense with the knife. Typical examples are switchblades, which can be carried concealed (and which are strongly forbidden in Germany) or the *karambit*, which actually comes from Asia. This agricultural implement has a claw-shaped blade and a finger ring.

TRIVIA: Ka-Bar: A Bear as a Namesake

We certainly don't want to pull anyone's leg, but the product from Union Cutlery Company that ultimately became the Ka-Bar did in fact have something to do with a bear. Unfortunately, it did not end well for the bear.

In the 1920s, a trapper of the Union Cutlery Company—who had marginal knowledge of English and sloppy handwriting, which made his account even more haunting—described how he was attacked by a wounded bear. Since his rifle had jammed, he reached for his knife. He described precisely how he used it to kill the bear ("kill a bear"). On the paper these words looked like "ka bar."

What a good story for a brand name! The leaders of the Union Cutlery Company thought so, and the Ka-Bar brand was born.

The Ronin II is a design by Michael Janich, founder of the Martial Blade Systems defense system.

Le Picoeur is a small, scalpel-like blade paired with a thin handle and pinky ring by Doug Marcaida and Bastinelli Knife. *Bastinelli*

Fred Perrin is an influential French close-combat expert. Here is his La Griffe, in the version made by Emerson Knives. *Emerson Knives*

A military classic: the Ka-Bar USMC

The Rogue Bowie (*top*) is an interpretation of the original Jim Bowie knife by American manufacturer Bark River. Its shape is claimed to be very authentic.

ORIGINAL BOWIE KNIFE

PRATHER WAR BOWIE
BY JEFF PRATHER

BOWIE KNIFE: The Knife of the Wild West

The man who gave his name to the notorious bowie knife is a Texas legend, an American folk hero, and almost a mythical figure. James Bowie was born in 1796 and lived a life marked by lust for adventure and bravado, drunkenness, slave trading, and land speculation. He is best known for his leading role in the Texas war of independence, during which Jim Bowie died in 1836.

When James Bowie was thirty years old he was wounded in a gunfight with Sheriff Norris Wright, and from then on at the latest he always carried a large knife with him. It is said to have been almost 10 inches long and had a blade almost 1.6 inches wide, and it may have been a gift from his brother Rezin Pleasant Bowie.

In 1827, Bowie and Wright faced each other again. The duel, which took place on a sandbank near Natchez, Mississippi, and in which each had seconds, got completely out of hand. Although the duel itself was over, shots were fired. In the following skirmish, Bowie suffered several bullet wounds and was cut and stabbed, yet he kept fighting. Wright was finally killed by Bowie's blade.

This incident, and other altercations in which Bowie fought with his knife, were so exaggerated by the press of the day that finally every "real man" wanted a knife like Bowie's. Exactly what Bowie's knife looked like is uncertain, but in the years after the sandbar fight the profile of the bowie knife became sharper. It is understood to have been a large and strong knife that typically had a clip point blade and a full guard.

Extravagant lines: the SOG Bowie 2.0 is reminiscent of the original Vietnam bowie knife used by special-unit MACV-SOG.

Alternative program to the bowie knife: a recommendation by influential woodcraft author Nessmuk.

Diving Knife

Beneath the surface of lakes and oceans is a largely unknown world. But it is not because of giant octopi, whose tentacles must be cut off to save oneself, or sharks, which can be driven off by stabbing them in the gills, that divers need a knife.

Ropes, lines, and nets do not catch just fish and marine mammals, but also divers. A diver whose legs or equipment become entangled in a loose fishing net (wrecks, in particular, are often covered with nets) can find themselves in serious difficulties. Diving knives are also regularly used for poking about and exploring, and for scraping and sending knocking signals. Professional divers need a knife that can be used as a lever, and with which they can cut even heavy rope; for example, if a hawser becomes entangled in a ship's propeller. A police diver reported that he once stuck his diving knife into the roof of a sunken automobile to be able to withstand the underwater current. It is important that the knife can be used even when one is wearing thick neoprene gloves, and that it has a good-fitting sheath.

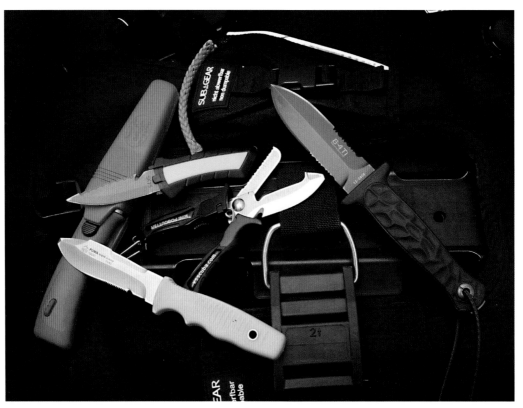

Underwater danger lurks primarily in the form of nets and lines, but diving knives are frequently also used for harvesting shellfish and other tasks.

Lying on the Torpedo throwing knife by Cold Steel are throwing knives by Elite Force, Walther, Cold Steel, and United Cutlery. The latter played a prominent role in the blockbuster *The Expendables*.

Throwing Knives

East Berlin: a British secret agent disguised as a clown flees a circus in the darkness. He is pursued by knife-throwing twins who obviously know what they are doing: 009 will not get far.

So much for the opening credits of the Bond film *Octopussy*, which some readers may associate with the subject of knife throwing. This is less a part of the secret agent's everyday routine than an exciting but, at the same time, relaxing hobby. The sound made by a knife tip striking wood is a satisfying one.

There are several things to consider when buying a throwing knife: the knife must be very sturdy, since it is exposed to enormous loads on impact. Great material strength and a not-too-thin blade are therefore trumps.

The blade steel and other materials should be tough, rather than particularly hard, if they are to stand up to their difficult job over time. A low-alloy, nonrustproof steel is a good choice.

The handle of a throwing knife must be shaped to provide a good grip position for the hand, which during the throw can be released smoothly. By the way, knives that are light and short do not fly as flat and straight as longer and heavier knives; hence the dictum "long works."

Because throwing knives frequently land on the ground, they should be easy to clean. Many manufacturers offer sets of knives, which makes a lot of sense.

SCAGEL & RANDALL: Influential to the Present Day

Bill Scagel

William "Bill" Scagel was born in Michigan in 1873. He was a fascinating personality, and the most influential knife maker of the early twentieth century. Bill Scagel first worked as a metalsmith, bridge builder, and woodworker in the forests of Canada. Around 1910, he began forging his own knives. In the 1920s, he opened his business Dogwood Nub, and from then on his main occupation was manufacturing knives, axes, pots, and boats. He sold his products mainly through Abercrombie & Fitch—then a large trader in outdoor and hunting equipment and not a fashion brand. Bill Scagel also equipped expedition teams with knives and chopping tools.

Word soon got around about Scagel's style and the high quality of his knives. The handles for his forged blades typically consisted of surroyal in the upper half, and the area near the grip of stacked leather discs. This construction became Scagel's trademark.

Bill Scagel's knives are therefore so popular that they greatly influenced another pioneer in American knives, Bo Randall.

Randall-Made Knives

In 1937, Bo Randall observed a man carrying out heavy repair work on his boots with a distinctive knife. He did this completely unhesitatingly, setting to work recklessly with this beautiful knife. Bo initially stood and watched, equally irritated and fascinated, finally buying the sturdy knife from the boot owner. It soon turned out that it was one of Bill Scagel's knives.

The first knife that Walter Doane "Bo" Randall completed in his hobby workshop in Orlando, Florida, was made from a file he reworked into a knife. Soon afterward, Randall set up a forge and worked tirelessly to make the best knife he could.

From the beginning, Bo Randall placed great value on clean lines and the uncompromising functionality of his knives, even though he still regarded knife making as a hobby. This did not change until 1941, when as a young marine Bo Randall was given the task of creating a versatile combat knife. This knife became so popular among the marine's fellow soldiers and friends that even the media reported about it.

The hymns of praise spread ever wider, and soon Randall was receiving letters with knife orders from all over the country. The "knife man from Florida" had done it, and his Model 1 All Purpose Fighter went into history. W. D. "Bo" Randall died on December 25, 1989. Since then, his son and his grandson have continued making knives in the traditional way.

William "Bill" Scagel was one of America's most influential knife makers. Here is a typical Scagel knife with surroyal handle and a forged blade.

Randall knives are made today almost the same way they were prior to the 1980s. Here is the beautiful Copper Companion with copper elements.

Chapter Summary

Knives with a blade permanently attached to the handle have been the most-important cutting tools for thousands of years. Their distribution is unbroken: in the kitchen, in outdoor activities, for hunting and military use, and wherever one must be able to depend to a special degree on their functionality and increased load capacity.

The significant criterion for distinguishing between fixed knives is the design of the tang and handle. There are flat-tang knives, fully and half-integral knives, and hidden-tang knives, such as Scandinavian knives.

The sheath is a decisive factor in the usability of a fixed knife. It is the sheath that makes it possible to carry the knife, have a good grip on it, and protect the wearer and equipment from the sharp and pointed blade. At the same time, the sheath protects the knife against damage, and especially loss. Beautifully made sheaths add to the visual appeal of a fixed knife. Among the most popular materials are leather and thermoplastic materials such as Kydex.

Fixed knives can be divided into seven significant classes. Hunting knives must be suitable for the many tasks in the wild, especially for cleaning game. Outdoor knives are among the most important items of equipment needed in the outdoors, and are used in particular for working with wood. Tactical and military knives have a similar requirements profile: they guarantee the survival of the user and are used mainly as versatile tools.

Self-defense knives are reduced to a single purpose: they are used solely to fight off an attacker. They must be sharp and pointed, quickly accessible, and safe to handle. Underwater dangers lurk for divers, especially in the shape of nets and lines in which they can become entangled. One can free oneself with a diving knife. And throwing knives are used mainly for enjoyment.

Made for the outdoors: dependable knives (here from Randall from the US and Svörd from New Zealand) are among the most important items of equipment in the wild.

There are many stages between the large Terävä Skrama (*second from left*) and the compact Taschenfixed from Schmiede Haselmayr (*far right*).

Chapter 3.
Chefs' Knives: From the
Kitchens of This World

All around the world, at this moment men and women are standing in front of their cutting boards, kitchen knife in hand. It is of essential significance for food preparation, whether it is a Chinese cleaver, a small Solingen peeling knife, or a chef's large cooking knife.

Like all good tools, chefs' knives must be perfectly oriented to their intended purpose: the efficient and precise cutting of food. Their function determines their form, which is essentially the same: every knife has a blade and a handle.

The details are determined by the preparation methods and by the food itself. Is it fish, meat, vegetables, or fruit? Must one cut around bones, or even split them? Must a hard peel be vanquished first to reach fine fruit flesh, or must fibrous flesh be divided with fine cuts to obtain the smoothest possible sections? Is the cutting being done freehand or on the board?

All these factors help determine what a chef's knife must look like. There is also cultural influence on the design, the handling, and the regard for chefs' knives.

Here you will learn everything you need to know about the important chefs' knives from Europe, Japan, and China.

The History of European Chefs' Knives

The Romans used eating daggers and forks, but over centuries this high state of development was forgotten. The first specialized cooking and preparation knives reappeared in Europe at the beginning of the late Middle Ages. The reason for this was the rapid development of cooking and culinary culture in the princely and royal courts of Italy and France. There were well-equipped kitchens, with cooks who had numerous cooking utensils at their disposal: grilling systems, ranges, pots and pans, and especially knives.

Before the food went to the kitchen, preparation work such as cleaning and peeling vegetables took place in the *salles d'office* by using short fixed knives, which are still important today and are mentioned in the French *Couteaux d'Office* (Paring Knives).

So-called blowhards (also called fore cutters) did their work at the table. In

The Parts of a European Chef's Knife

1. Point
2. Blade
3. Edge / cutting edge
4. Beard
5. Spine
6. Blade lettering
7. Bolster
   (often integral and forged)
8. Hand guard
9. Handle fasteners
10. Handle
11. Butt

Some of the best-known knife makers in the world still produce their products in Solingen, Germany. At Herder and other companies, they are again hard at work on the next generation of knives.

addition to professionally dismantling large pieces of meat, they were also responsible for entertaining guests.

The best pieces of meat were distributed according to rank. Woe to the "blowhard" who made a faux pas doing this, or in conversing with the guests.

With the French Revolution at the end of the eighteenth century, the cooks who worked in the courts lost their jobs. The ones who did not return to their families in the country opened inns and restaurants in the cities. As a result, the "nouvelle cuisine" practiced in the courts spread throughout the entire country.

And so cooking and eating customs changed, as did the need for specially suited equipment: the triumphal march of the chef's knife began, and the then-leading centers of knife manufacture adapted to meet the new demand.

The Centers of
European Knife Production

French influence on the development of European cooking-knife culture is enormous. Despite this, Germany took a leading role, especially with knives made in Solingen: Zwilling J. A. Henckels was once the largest cutlery factory in the world. The distinctive twins emblem was already a trademark of the Solingen knife maker in 1731. Around 1900, the Zwilling production program included about 10,000 different articles, especially pocketknives.

The history of the Ed. Wüsthof company goes back to the beginning of the nineteenth century. Its trident is one of the best-known trademarks on blades. Wüsthof also formerly produced hundreds of different pocketknife models. Today the company specializes in the production of cooking and household knives. One of its most important markets is the United States.

Güde—a cutlery company founded in Solingen in 1910—made cooking-knife history when Franz Güde, son of company founder Karl Güde, submitted the serrated edge for patent. Production at Güde, which involves a high proportion of manual work, is in part reminiscent of the times when the company was founded.

Representative of other German manufacturers—which produce cooking knives in Solingen with a high proportion of manual work, passion, involvement, and expertise—is Robert Herder GmbH & Co., which was founded in 1872.

For those who do not recognize the name Herder, perhaps the name Windmill Knives and the corresponding logo will ring a bell. There the tradition of the Solingen precision grind is held high, in which the blades are very finely ground and polished (traditional fine honing methods are still practiced there). The company has also gained a high level of expertise in the field of Asiatic knives.

Among the best-known makers of chefs' knives in France are Atelier Percival and the

The big chef's knife is the star of every kitchen. Victorinox offers a good-cutting drop-forged version with a beautiful rosewood handle. The Yvo 1 is the chef's knife from the knife maker in Hohenmoor.

VICTORINOX

7.7400.20

KING DELUXE STONE 1200

traditional manufacturer Sabatier: in the French forging capital of Thiers, Philippe Sabatier made cooking knives for the kitchens of the courts. His descendents have continued his business for eight generations.

The town of Scarperia is near Florence, Italy. There, too, the tradition of making knives by hand can be traced back to the Middle Ages. The Coltellerie Berti (since 1895), Coltellerie Consiglu, and Coltellerie Saladini companies produce not only historic Italian pocketknives, but also a selection of beautiful cooking knives.

Characteristics
of Western Chefs' Knives

Germany is known worldwide primarily for integral knives, whose bolster (the thickening at the transition between the blade and handle), tang, and pommel are made from one and the same piece of steel. Also typically European is the preference for rustproof steel. They are usually not as extremely hardened as those made in Japan. The blades from these manufacturers are often not quite as thin and finely ground as those in Japan.

As a result, European knives do not have the same cutting properties as their Japanese colleagues. They are sturdier. As a general rule, European knives are partially ground on both sides; consequently, the blade flanks come together at the cutting edge at the same angle.

The Most-Important
Knives in Western Kitchens
The Chef's Cooking Knife

At the very top of our professional kitchen is the master chef, the *chef de cuisine*. His edged counterpart is the chef's cooking knife: in the hands of a professional, the long *couteau de chef* becomes a jack of all trades, cutting meat and vegetables, mincing herbs, filleting fish, and breaking open and dividing shellfish such as large lobster. Typically the blade length is between 7 and 12 inches, though most professionals tend to use a knife with a 9.5-inch blade. Such cooks tend to have the necessary freedom of movement in their kitchens and sufficiently large cutting boards.

A typical feature of a chef's cooking knife is a relatively tall blade. The distance between the cutting edge and the blade spine is often up to 2 inches. These high blade flanks provide a good grip and, while cutting with the typical claw grip, ensure excellent control along the knuckles. They can be used—including the spine with its edges—for special tasks, such as peeling garlic cloves or cracking the shells of crustaceans.

Blade height is also important when working on a cutting board; it creates so much free space beneath the handle that even the knuckles of the knife-guiding hand do not touch the cutting board if one is using the rearmost part of the blade. The broad blade is also best suited for lifting and positioning the sliced food.

The blade extends in a gentle arc to the tip, so the full length of the blade can be used in drawing cuts when working on a cutting board. The curved cutting edge also makes it suitable for rocking cuts and for chopping.

Kitchen and Larding Knives

After the chef comes the *sous-chef*. Or put another way: if the chef's big cooking knife is the king of the kitchen, then kitchen and larding knives are his knights.

The two types of pointed knife are used for all small cutting jobs that may come up: peeling vegetables, mushrooms, and fruit; carving, cutting, and trimming; removing stems, cores, and bad spots; removing the membranes and veins from goose liver; and much more. In households without chef's cooking knives they also take over its functions.

The difference between kitchen and larding knives is primarily the length of the blade. The kitchen knife typically has a blade between 2.75 and 3.5 inches long, while those of larding knives are between 3.5 and 6 inches in length.

The kitchen knife has its origins in the *salles d'office* anterooms of the courtly kitchens of the French aristocracy. All the necessary preparatory work was carried out there. In the past, larding knives were used to "lard" lean roast meat, making cuts into which bacon was inserted. Nowadays special needles are used for this task, but the name has remained.

Versions of the kitchen knife are also called Kneipchen, Hümmeken, or Zöppken, or Pittermesser or Schneidteufelchen in Germany. In different regions these knives have a variety of blade types and shapes. Most are very handy and easy to use.

Filleting Knife

The object of filleting is to remove the delicacies—the filets. Filleting is usually understood to mean removing the fleshy side pieces from fish, separating the flesh from the bones and skin. The knife must be very sharp and long enough. European filleting knives are always flexible to a certain degree, requiring a relatively thin, toughly hardened blade.

The fibrous, delicate flesh of fishes presents a challenge and does not allow a dull blade. Only if they have smooth cut surfaces and are in one piece do fish filets look the way they should: appetizing. Filleting knives should therefore be pedantically kept at maximum sharpness. The larger the fish, the larger the blade should be. If the blade is sharp and also long, one can proceed effectively with a few drawing cuts and not have to saw back and forth so often. Filleting knives are also sometimes coated to reduce friction while cutting.

Blade lengths up to 8 inches have proven effective, but many cooks swear by even-longer formats. Most slim and flexible blades suit the task and are easy to use. In some cases the flexible blades are also used slightly bent.

Incidentally, not only fish are filleted—the exact removal of the fine flesh of citrus fruits is also called filleting. This too is best done with a long, sharp blade.

Filleting knife from WMF of Germany with a forged 1.4116 stainless-steel blade. *WMF*

The rubber handle and coating also make this filleting knife from Martini of Finland of interest to fishermen. *Martini*

Giesser of Germany manufactures a variety of knives for use in professional kitchens and in private households. Here is a basic series model with a walnut handle. *Giesser*

Suitable for any job—kitchen and larding knives are the sweepers of every kitchen and are used for a multitude of tasks.

Deboning Knife—the Curve Cutter

The name "deboning knife" says it all. The bones are the bones of animals, which we want to separate from the flesh. For this purpose, most deboning knives have a thin, flexible blade that is not too long, with the cutting edge extending in an arc to the tip. With this maneuverable blade one can easily follow the windings of the bone structure and work precisely in close conditions.

A deboning knife typically has a large guard. It prevents the hand from sliding onto the sharp blade when cutting if the tip abruptly strikes a bone and becomes stuck.

The deboning knife is a typical butcher's tool, but it is also an indispensable assistant in fine kitchens when large fish or whole lambs are being worked on. Even in home kitchens the deboning knife is well suited for separating bones and removing fat, sinews, and the skin from small animals and poultry.

Bread Knife

The bread knife is at home not just at the breakfast or dinner table. It has long found a place in professional kitchens, where it is used to cut hard-skinned fruit and vegetable varieties such as pineapples, melons, quinces, pomegranates, artichokes, and squash.

The blade of a bread knife can be very long. It should even be as long as possible—in any case longer than the widest loaf of bread one wants to cut. And so manufacturers even offer knives with blades longer than 12 inches.

The cutting edge of a bread knife is serrated instead of straight: the sharpened serrations grip better and prevent slipping, are relatively durable, and also cut through the hardest bread crust, and so prepare the slice. This is taken over by the more finely ground inner radii, which separate the individual outer serrations from one another. Because of this blade profile they are also

A slip-proof handle is an especially important part of a deboning knife. The blade is used to separate meat from bones. *Victorinox*

A pastry knife from Victorinox and a long-serving bread knife from Herder. With their serrated blades they cut not only bread but also hard-skinned fruits and vegetables.

The fish-rich waters of Japan and its diversity of foods have resulted in the development of specialized cooking knives.

One of the specialities of the Japanese cooking knife giant Kai—to which the knife brands Kershaw and Zero Tolerance also belong—is the *suminagashi* blade.

referred to as bread saws. A precisely made bread saw is more than just a nice extra.

The History of
the Japanese Cooking Knife

The oldest cooking knife found in Japan dates to the eighth century. The Nara period, which extended over much of this century, was a time of upheavals. And the Chinese culture particularly left its mark on many aspects of Japanese life: the development of the script, the spread of Buddhism, and the modernization of the political system.

It was not just the swords wielded by Japanese warriors that originally came from China or were produced against the Chinese example. The first Japanese cooking knives also showed Chinese influence, but something special developed from these "cribbed" beginnings: the bladed weapons of the Japanese samurai have become legendary, and Japanese cooking knives are just as versatile as they are aesthetic and uncompromising.

Among the most-important knife-making centers in Japan are Sakai, Takefu, Kyuto, and Seki. Sakai is near Osaka, an important trade center. Swords have been made in Sakai since the fourteenth century, and the production of steel knives began in the sixteenth century.

The Portuguese brought tobacco to Japan. Initially, the knives made in Sakai were primarily for processing tobacco. Traditional Japanese cooking knives followed soon after. Even today, Sakai remains the most important production center for the classic cooking knife of Japan, the so-called *wa-bocho*. This can also be traced to its proximity to Osaka and Kyuto. Both are traditional centers of Japanese culinary culture.

Like Sakai, Takefu is a location strongly oriented toward craftsmanship and has a long tradition of knife making. Kyuto—the oldest imperial city in Japan—no longer plays a major role, but historically it was an important forging location for carbon-steel knives.

Worldwide, Seki is the best-known name when it comes to Japanese blades. In the country itself, Seki is a high-technology center for manufacturing industrial knives and household knives, but also high-grade knives for export.

Among the best-known knife makers in Japan is the Kai Company, which was founded in Seki in 1908. The company initially made pocketknives and razor blades, and it was not until 1971 that it began making the cooking knives for which Kai is well known. Many knives from the Kai range are made according to the so-called *suminagashi* pattern. A centrally positioned cutting edge of very hardened and wearproof steel is flanked by overlays of different types of steel. This provides an attractive Damascus steel look in combination with high cutting performance. *Suminagashi* means something like "ink floating," referring to an ancient Japanese technique of painting on water.

Industrial knife manufacturers such as Global, Tojiro, Mizuno, and Kanetsune are also popular in Europe and are readily available. Occasionally, passionate dealers also secure products from small-batch production by Japanese manufacturers.

Typical Features of Japanese Cooking Knives

In addition to industrial production, which is essentially similar to that in Europe, in Japan there is a clearly greater distribution of smaller manufacturers. These forge the traditional Japanese cooking knife, the *wa-bocho*. *Wa* is associated with a traditional Japanese stylistic direction. *Bocho*, or also *hocho*, means knife.

Unlike Western cooking knives, handle scales, a pommel, or tangs extending to the end of the handle are not present on traditional Japanese knives. Instead, the handle, which frequently consists of two parts made of horn and magnolia wood, is simply glued to the knife's tang. As a result, Japanese knives are usually much lighter and top heavy than Western knives.

A *wa-bocho*—whose blade consists of a single piece of steel, which in the area of the cutting edge is hardened more than the rest—is called *honyaki*. If the blade is made of two or three layers of core-steel (*hagane*) and softer cladding (*jigane*), it is a *kasumi* knife.

Typically Japanese is the preference for nonrustproof steel, which is hardened to an extremely high degree and is ground especially fine and thin. Extremely fine cuts are possible with these highly developed cutting tools. The blades also retain their sharpness for a very long time. They are clearly more delicate than Western knives and cannot endure any kind of mistreatment. Even the accidental striking of a bone or a cutting board can result in damage. To prevent the blades from rusting, they must be cleaned after each use. Japanese cooks often have a damp cloth right next to the cutting board, wiping the blade every few seconds.

Most *wa-bocho* blades are ground on one side; then they are called *kataba*. Knives ground on both sides are called *ryoba* and are classed as *yobocho*: these are modern Japanese knives influenced by Western culture (*yo* = modern/Western) and are often manufactured industrially.

The Most-Important Japanese Cooking Knives
Yanagiba

The *yanagiba* is one of the traditional Japanese knives (*wa-bocho*) and is usually produced from nonrustproof steel. It is a long, slender knife used primarily to prepare sashimi: an especially demanding preparation method for raw fish. The precision and fineness of the cuts is a decisive factor in the flavor and aesthetic enjoyment.

Some professional Japanese cooks use blades with lengths in excess of 14 inches. The combination of fine blade geometry and the very sharp grind make it possible to thinly filet the delicate fish by making only a few cuts. Using its entire length, the single-bevel blade is drawn through the flesh in a pulling movement. There are different versions of the *yanagiba* for different kinds

Photo: *Gourmet Connection*

Parts of the Japanese Cooking Knife
1. *Kissaki* (point)
2. *Hasaki* (cutting edge)
3. *Kiriha* (bevel)
4. *Shinogisuji* (bevel grind)
5. *Ago* (sharp-edged end of the blade)
6. *Tsukamoto* (exposed tang)
7. *Kakumaki* (bolster, often made of horn)
8. *Tsuka* (handle)
9. *Tsukajiri* (butt)

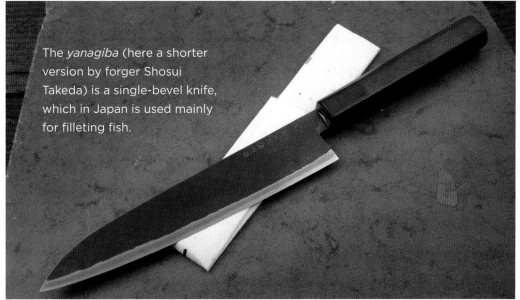

The *yanagiba* (here a shorter version by forger Shosui Takeda) is a single-bevel knife, which in Japan is used mainly for filleting fish.

of fish: the thinner *fuguhiki* is preferred for preparing blowfish (fugu).

Usuba

The *usuba* is a specialized *wa-bocho* used for the precise cutting and decoration of vegetables. The Japanese kitchen is known for razor-thin radish slices that become hard as nails in a cold water bath. The *usuba* is also used to make these.

Usuba stands for "thin slice," and the name says it all. The non-stainless-steel blade of a *usuba* is very thin and tall compared to other types of Japanese knife. The blade is chisel-ground at a very fine angle—always from the right for right-handers (view from above toward the knife in the hand). The cutting edge is straight, so that its full length rests on the cutting board.

All of this makes the finest cuts possible, making the knife able to cut through firm vegetables without cracking them.

The area of the blade near the handle is used to cut food, while the central area of the cutting edge is very well suited to peeling vegetables. The forward blade area and the Usuba's sharp edge make it an effective tool for precise, decorative cuts.

Nakiri

The *nakiri* is a traditional knife for peeling, cutting, and chopping vegetables. The blade is thin, and the cutting edge is straight, or minimally curved. In contrast to most other *wa-bocho*, it has a double-bevel blade and is used primarily with vertical pressure, rather than a drawing cut.

The *nakiri* is nearly rectangular, either with an angular tip or a slightly rounded one depending on region. The broad blade is well suited to cut vegetables. Despite its similarity to a real chopping knife, because of its fine blade geometry the *nakiri* is suitable only for cutting soft foods—never for slicing or cutting through bones.

Deba

With its wide spine and high weight, this traditional Japanese *deba* is made for chopping through bones, for cutting off and dismantling fish heads, and for removing tail fins. In this case, chopping does not mean a striking movement, but rather a powerful pushing one. At most, one strikes the spine of the blade with a balled fist. The *deba* is also used for finer work, such as removing gills and filleting.

The blade of a *deba* is usually forged using the *awase* (cladding) technique: high-carbon steel forms a hard cutting edge, whereas the layer of softer steel or iron makes the spine strong and resistant to cracking and chipping.

The knife has a single-bevel blade and is normally between 4.7 and 9.4 inches long. The area of the blade near the *deba*'s handle is used for cutting through bones, and the forward area is for cutting and filleting.

Gyuto

The *gyuto* is a *yobocho* (the modern knives of Japan influenced by Western culture). It is a Japanese variant of the French chef knife. Roughly translated, the name means beef

The name *usuba* essentially means "thin blade." The Kama-Usuba (with gray magnolia handle) and the Kai Shun Pro Sho Usuba (*bottom*) skillfully put this premise into practice.

The *nakiri* is a specialist for cutting vegetables. Although it is a *wa-bocho*, it has a double bevel. This model is forged by Hohenmoorer in Germany.

THE CHINESE COOKING KNIFE: One for All

The Chinese kitchen offers much that is unknown and an always recurring knife: the traditional, uniquely shaped Chinese cooking knife, which is known internationally as the *cai dao* (vegetable knife), or Chinese cleaver.

As in Japan, Chinese culinary culture has been highly developed for thousands of years. Also as in Japan, the cutting of ingredients plays a very important role in cooking. What we merely call cooking is in Chinese *ge peng*, or cutting and cooking. Both are inseparably linked. And yet, despite its many regional cuisines and its long cooking history, the Chinese kitchen is dominated by a single type of knife.

With its wide, up to 4.7-inch-tall blade, the Chinese cooking knife is used to dismember huge crabs or cut vegetables into razor-thin slices. The broad flanks gently pound meat soft, help cloves of garlic lose their skins with a light tap, provide good guidance along a bone, and shovel the food into the pan. Earlier, when there was often just one knife per household, it was also used to break bones—part of a Chinese meat dish—and even prepare firewood.

There is almost nothing that the curiously shaped knife cannot do in the hands of a gifted cook. Cooks who have become used to handling it often don't want to do without it. No wonder—what other knife is capable of carrying out so many jobs?

At first glance the Chinese cooking knife looks like a meat cleaver. Modern versions are clearly more elegant.

knife. Like the chef's cooking knife, it is used as a universal knife. That is not the only parallel: the *gyuto* and the chef's cooking knife are also similar in blade length (7 to 10.5 inches) and grind (double bevel). There are *gyuto* knives with Western handle designs, with a continuous flat tang, and Japanese versions with a hidden tang. In most cases the *gyuto* is more heavily tuned for good cutting qualities than the chef's cooking knife from Europe, with finer blade geometry and more tempered steel. It requires somewhat greater caution during use.

Santoku

The *santoku* is one of the most popular Japanese knives—especially in Europe, but also in many private residences in Japan. Like the *gyuto*, it is a Western-inspired double-bevel cooking knife.

The name is a play on the "three virtues." Many see this as a reflection of its suitability for cutting meat, fish, and vegetables. Other interpretations relate to its ability to be used for pulling and pushing cuts and for chopping. The three blade areas—the tip (for fine cuts), the main length of the cutting edge (for a variety of cutting tasks), and the

The *deba* by Hideo Kitaoka (*top*) relies on two layers of steel; the *deba* by Kai is etched VG-10 steel.

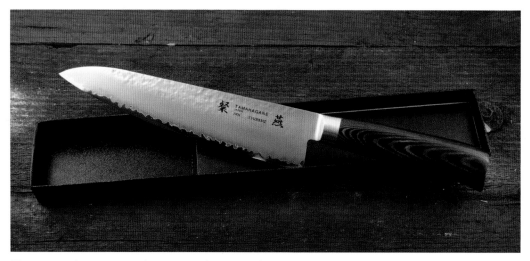

The *gyuto*, here a *tamahagane tsubame* in the San-Mai version, is the Japanese interpretation of the European cooking knife.

TRIVIA: RECOMMENDATION: Three Knives That One Needs

An ambitious amateur is well equipped with just three types of knife: the chef's cooking knife, the larding or kitchen knife, and the bread knife are the big three of the kitchen. Of course their Japanese counterparts are also suitable.

For kitchen professionals, the chef's large cooking knife is the most versatile and important knife. It is capable of carrying out the majority of cutting tasks very well. There are differences in bolster design with which one should be familiar. Especially on drop-forged knives from Germany, the heel—the trailing edge of the blade at the handle—is left thick and is not sharpened. If one's hand slips forward while working, one does not cut oneself so easily. This type of blade makes sharpening more difficult, since the heel should also be ground to exactly maintain the line of the cutting edge. French-style chefs' cooking knives usually have a round bolster without a thickened heel. Japanese knives frequently dispense with a bolster entirely and always sharpen the blade over its entire length. The sharp heel is thus ready to scratch rinds or to remove bad spots.

For those who wish, there are also special knives with which one can work even more precisely and with more joy and pleasure; the selection is huge.

heel (the rear part of the blade, suitable for high-pressure cuts)—are seen as virtues. The *santoku* is simply a true all-rounder.

Chapter Summary

In Europe, the manufacture and use of knives has a tradition extending back to the late Middle Ages and has its origins in Italian and French courts. From these beginnings, many specialized models have developed. Among the most-important European cooking knives are the chef's cooking knife, kitchen knife, and bread knife.

The variety of knives available in Japan is incomparably greater. Nowhere else does the *hocho* (knife) have such status. There the cooking knife is the "soul of the cook," and there is a unique knife for every special preparation method.

And in China, cooking is inseparably associated with the cutting of food. A single type of knife, the Chinese cleaver or *cai dao*, dominates the entire land—this despite the many different regional cuisines of China and its long cultural history.

The *santoku* is considered an all-around in the kitchen. Here is a Swiss variant with a fluted edge.

Chapter 4. Folding Knives: The Friend in the Pocket

The oldest known folding knife comes from the archeologically significant Hallstatt period (Early Iron Age, western and central Europe, eighth to fifth centuries BCE) and is easily 2,500 years old. The Celtic piece has an iron blade. There is also a multipiece and multifunctional tool and cutlery knife—made of silver, with a spoon, fork, and toothpick—dating from the third century. It was possibly carried by a well-to-do Roman during his travels. The pattern books of the big knife manufacturers of the eighteenth and nineteenth centuries contain hundreds of different models of pocketknife, from fine gentlemen's knives to specialized folding knives for work and hunting. The number of models is not as great today, but it is still impressive.

Folding knives are always a good choice when compact packing size is important: despite a fully adequate handle, a 3.15-inch-long blade can easily fit into a pants pocket, which is usually 4.3 inches deep. That is unbeatable. Folding knives are also especially safe to transport, since in folded condition the sharp blade point and cutting edge are completely separated. Compared to fixed knives, because of their large number of parts and the necessary mechanism, folding knives usually require more care and are not as durable.

Folding Aids

Nail Mark and Blade Spine

Folding knives differ in how the blade is extended and folded again. This can be done in the traditional way, with two hands. In addition to a blade spine extending far out of the handle, the most common opening aid on two-handed knives is the so-called nail mark. It is a groove in the side of the blade that provides secure footing for a thumbnail when opening the knife. Most traditional folding knives are of this two-hand type, including style legends such as the Buck 110.

Automatic Knives

Mankind has always sought ways to achieve its goals as comfortably as possible. And if the goal is to use a folding knife, then there is no more comfortable choice than an automatic knife. Such flick knives were already being made in the middle of the eighteenth century by hand for a small circle of users.

In the mid-nineteenth century, the cutlery industry in Sheffield, England, began mass-

Parts of the Folding Knife

1. Blade point
2. Cutting edge
3. Grind (hollow, flat, or grind)
4. Ricasso
5. One-hand opening aid (here Spyderco finger choil)
6. Thumb ramp
7. False edge
8. Handle
9. Back lock release
10. Pocket clip

Automatic knife: a spiral spring is wound around the blade axis. When the blade is closed, the spring is under tension. If one presses the release button on the handle, the blade pops out.

producing automatic knife models. The Solingen Springer (known as Lever Lock in English) is described and illustrated in manufacturers' catalogues produced before 1900.

At the end of the nineteenth century, "automatic fever" also gripped the US thanks to the meeting of George Schrade and the Walden Knife Company. At the beginning of the twentieth century, production of the *coltello scatto* (snapper knife) began in Maniago, Italy. Without one of these Italian stilettos, the James Dean classic *For They Know Not What They Do* might not have become so legendary.

The automatic knife makers' target group did not include just glove-wearing workers, farmers, and hunters, but also women; finely manicured nails could not be expected to deal with a nail mark and powerful spine spring.

Thumb Stud, Flipper & Co.

One-hand knives—as they are known to-day—appeared in the mid-1970s. The thumb pin marked the beginning. When the Spyderco Company developed the Worker in 1981, it was something of a revolution: the blade could be opened with one hand by using a circular cutout in the blade (which to this day remains Spyderco's trademark). The knife could also be attached to the pants with the clip.

The blade of a flipper knife is formed in such a way that a short lever extends from the handle when the blade is folded. If one pulls back on this with one's pointer finger, the blade is ejected. This requires an easy-operating blade, accomplished with ball bearings.

Locking Mechanisms

The first folding knives were manufactured for more than 200 years. These early knives were kept open mainly by the friction on the handle scales. Then, in the middle of the seventeenth century, operating safety took a huge step forward. The development of constantly reproducible spring steel made it possible to make folding knives with a spine spring-locking mechanism. After this, blade-locking methods appeared in vast numbers.

Friction Folder

The simplest of all folding knives needs just a blade, pin, and handle. Folded, the blade rests in the handle cutout. Opened, the end of the blade strikes the handle or, if the blade spine has been lengthened into a lever, opens onto the handle. More-complex designs of so-called friction folders have a separate stop for the blade or consist of multipart handle designs.

There is generally no blade lock mechanism or spring. The friction between the blade and the inner sides of the handle prevents the blade from too easily opening or closing. To the present day, this type of knife is popular mainly in France (Piemontais) and Japan (*higonokami*).

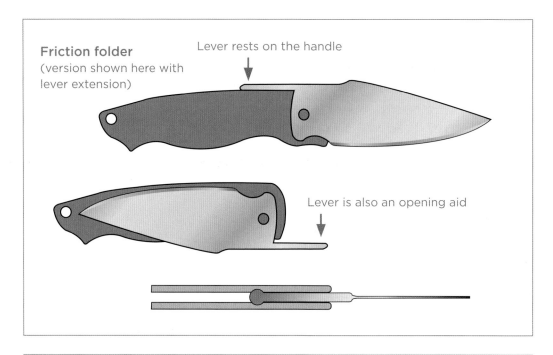

Friction folder
(version shown here with
lever extension)

Lever rests on the handle

Lever is also an opening aid

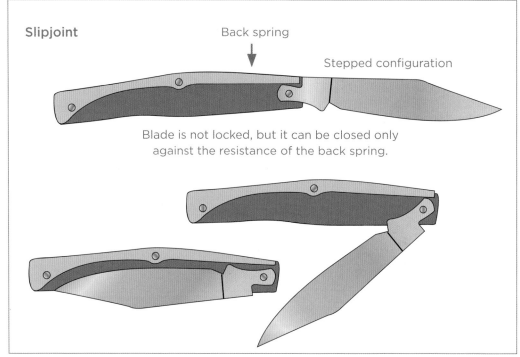

Slipjoint

Back spring

Stepped configuration

Blade is not locked, but it can be closed only
against the resistance of the back spring.

Slip Joint

Pocketknives whose blades are prevented from folding by a back spring have been around for about 250 years. This folding-knife design (slip joint) was made possible by the development of spring steel in the mid-seventeenth century.

The blade of a slip joint knife is not locked, but it is at least actively held in place. It is held in place in the handle, or in working position by a spring in the back of the handle, which usually presses into a step-shaped receptacle in the root of the blade. French versions had a derivation of this classic design, the spring having a small hammerhead that engages a specially formed slot in the blade root, so more force is required to fold the knife.

The best-known example of a knife with a back spring and no lock is the Swiss Army Knife, but garden knives, cowboy jackknives, and regional knives of France for the most part rely on similar mechanisms.

Viroblock

The best-known knife with a locking collar is a French export success: Opinel places the blade in a one-piece wooden handle, the blade end of which is round. A metal clamping band is first placed on it. The pivot pin passes through this clamping band and thus forms two hold points for a rotating and slotted locking collar: the so-called viroblock.

If one turns the viroblock, its upper edge pushes in front of the slot and prevents the

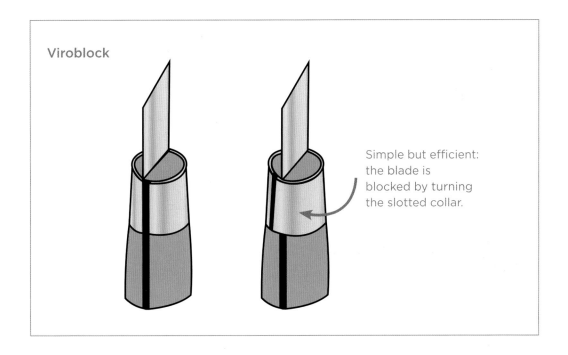

Viroblock

Simple but efficient: the blade is blocked by turning the slotted collar.

blade from folding. Nontron—one of the oldest of all French knife manufacturers—adopted a similar locking-collar mechanism in the mid-seventeenth century! The locking collar is thus one of the oldest locking mechanisms for folding knives.

Back Lock

A folding knife whose blade is secured by a dependable mechanism is especially safe to handle. One such locking mechanism is the back lock (also written backlock or lock-back). When it was invented is uncertain, but it was probably in the nineteenth century.

It became popular with the Model 110 Folding Hunter by American manufacturer Buck Knives. It came on the market in 1964, and since then it has embedded itself in the universal knife consciousness like no other folding knife. In addition to the typical components such as a blade, axis pin, and handle, it also has a multipiece locking mechanism. The lock part is made of steel, the front end of which forms a hammerhead. A correspondingly shaped nut is in the tang.

When the knife is open, a spring in the end of the handle presses the lock lever forward into the tang nut. To release this connection, the other end of the lock lever must be pressed against the force of the spring in the handle, causing the hammerhead to pivot upward.

When the blade is closed, the hammerhead (of the lock lever) presses (again by the power of the spring) on an edge of the underside of the tang. This prevents the blade from inadvertently folding out of the handle.

On most lock back knives the lock lever also forms the stop of the extended blade. An exception is a variant of the back lock called the Tri-Ad Lock, developed by Andrew Demko and produced in quantity by Cold Steel. It has a stop pin, making the design even stronger.

Liner Lock

In the nineteenth century there were already folding knives whose blades were locked in position by a side-spring lock. With the blade in the open position, a blocking plate sprang into position behind the tang, and the blade could not be folded again until this plate was pushed out of the way. A conventional back spring was used as a blade stop—and to hold the folded blade in the handle. While reliable, this mechanism, which is sometimes still used today, was not as easy to use, precise, and free of play as the modern liner lock.

The development of the liner lock was due to Michael Walker, who had worked as a knifesmith starting in the mid-1970s and invented more than twenty locking mechanisms. The best known and widely used of these is the liner lock, which he developed in 1981. With the correct design and precise construction, it is very sturdy and reliable: to lock the extended blade, a lock bar snaps into place directly behind the

Back lock

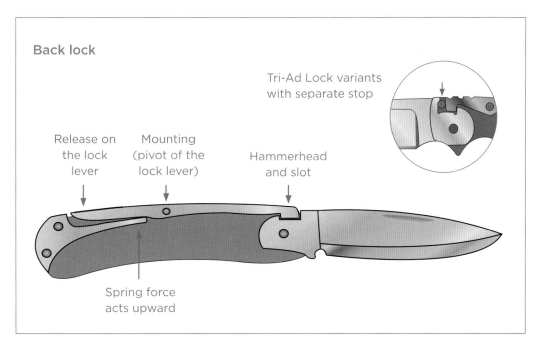

Tri-Ad Lock variants with separate stop

Release on the lock lever

Mounting (pivot of the lock lever)

Hammerhead and slot

Spring force acts upward

Liner lock

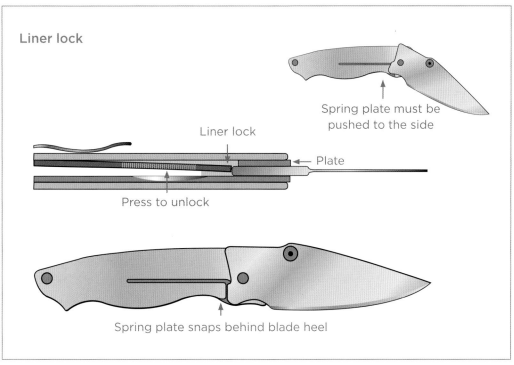

Spring plate must be pushed to the side

Liner lock

Plate

Press to unlock

Spring plate snaps behind blade heel

tang. This spring can be placed in the handle as a separate part. More commonly it is an integral part of a metal lock bar. The bar is cut and bent in such a way that the section springs to the side, strikes the sloping blade ramp, and presses the blade against the stop pin. To fold the blade, one must press the locking spring to the side.

A detent ball—a small steel sphere that sits in the locking spring—is usually used to hold the folded blade in the handle. It snaps into a small recess in the tang and holds the blade.

Frame Lock

The frame lock—first used by South African knifesmith Chris Reeve in his bestselling Sebenza model in 1981—is a variant of the liner lock. Here the locking spring is not part of a separate locking bar; instead it is formed by one of the two titanium-handle halves. This is notched lengthwise and so tensioned that it springs behind the blade end as soon as the blade is fully extended. There its end strikes the bevel of the blade axis. To be able to fold the blade into the handle, the locking spring must be pushed outward—like the liner lock. But compared to the liner lock, the frame lock's locking spring is clearly stronger.

More and more manufacturers are producing the locking-spring stop pin as a separate, replaceable part—especially if the locking spring is made of titanium or aluminum, since these materials are clearly softer than the steel blade tang. This counteracts wear.

TRIVIA: LAWKS:
Double Safe

Michael Walker and Ron Lake developed an additional safety for the liner lock. The mechanism, called the LAWKS (Lake And Walker Knife Safety), also blocks the locking spring. To fold the blade, first the locking spring and then the safety switch have to be pushed to the side.

Button Lock

The button lock is often found on automatic knives—but not just there. The central element is a locking bolt that passes through one of the handle scales. It is positioned on the blade heel so that it blocks the blade.

The bolt—against the force of a spring seated in the other half of the handle—can be pushed some way into the handle. Then a cutout in the bolt moves so far down that the blade heel can pass through it and the blade is released.

Folding-Knife Classics

The world of folding knives is varied. Many countries have managed to establish certain types of knives that are considered typical of their country.

The Swiss

For many centuries, Swiss pocketknives have been manufactured—officially and unofficially—by two Swiss companies: the fam-

Frame lock

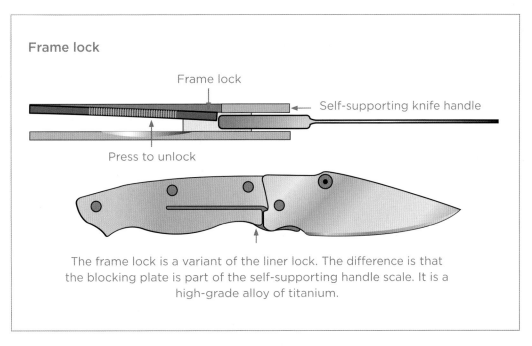

Frame lock

Self-supporting knife handle

Press to unlock

The frame lock is a variant of the liner lock. The difference is that the blocking plate is part of the self-supporting handle scale. It is a high-grade alloy of titanium.

Button lock

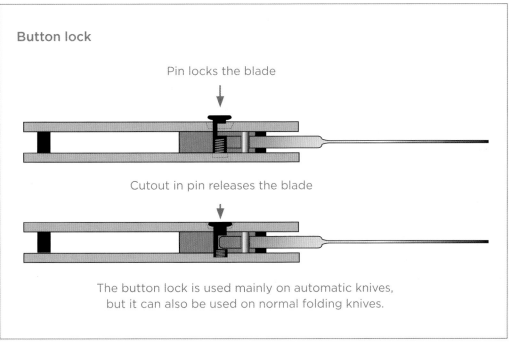

Pin locks the blade

Cutout in pin releases the blade

The button lock is used mainly on automatic knives, but it can also be used on normal folding knives.

ily firm Victorinox from Ibach and Wenger from Delémont, in the canton of Jura. Typical of both is a red handle with the Swiss Cross and very high quality at a moderate price. Today only Victorinox continues to produce the official Swiss Pocket Knife.

Karl Elsener, who founded Victorinox, opened a knife-manufacturing company in 1884 to provide the Swiss army with a reliable folding knife for use by its soldiers. He succeeded in 1890, and to this day the Swiss Army Knife comes from Victorinox. After this first great success, Elsener worked for years on another revolutionary idea: a compact knife offering many functions. On June 12, 1897, he legally protected his elegant, light, and versatile Officer's Knife and Sport Knife. Together these two models still form the foundation of the current Victorinox catalog. They are supported by a large number of other pocket tools, accessories, and true multitools.

The Officer's Knife from Victorinox can be found in many museums around the world—such as the New York Museum of Modern Art and the State Museum of Applied Art in Munich—as a design classic. Long ago the Swiss knife also achieved classic status in popular culture. The American television show *MacGyver*, from the 1980s, made it a symbol of inventiveness and functionality. The Swiss Army Knife has even gone to space, and on its home page NASA officially recommends it as a supplementary item of equipment for its astronauts. Swiss quality is relied on—always and everywhere.

German Folding Knives

The question of a typical German folding knife is not so simple to answer, since in Solingen, knives have always been produced for the entire world. For example, one model built there as a backup combat or general-purpose knife was called the Sodbuster in the US.

Technically at least, there is no German equivalent to the typical Swiss knife. Functionally there is, since the first Swiss army knives in fact came from Solingen. They were produced there until Victorinox founder Karl Elsener took control. Today the Solingen manufacturer Böker produces the Sport Knife, a model that is very similar to the military knife offered before 1900.

The Solingen Lever Lock Springer, which is still produced in large numbers by Hubertus, must also be considered typically German, as are the one-part to multipart folding hunting knives with deer horn scales from manufacturers such as Puma or Diefenthal.

Solingen manufacturers Friedrich Hartkopf and Robert Klaas still have classic one-part and multipart knives in their range that are basic equipment for many people: simple but good knives for everyday use and meal time.

Traditional manufacturers Löwen (C. Lütters & Cie.) and Otter have an excellent reputation at home and abroad among collectors, and especially among users from the technical and maritime fields. Among the most well-known products from these two companies is the Anchor Knife, which has an inlayed anchor on one of the handle halves

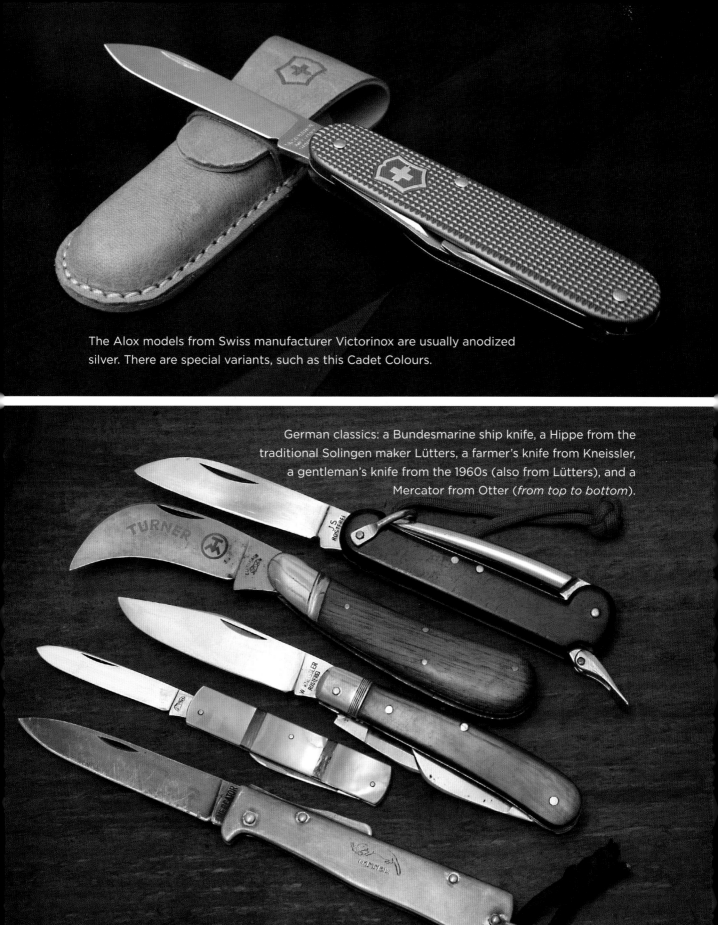

The Alox models from Swiss manufacturer Victorinox are usually anodized silver. There are special variants, such as this Cadet Colours.

German classics: a Bundesmarine ship knife, a Hippe from the traditional Solingen maker Lütters, a farmer's knife from Kneissler, a gentleman's knife from the 1960s (also from Lütters), and a Mercator from Otter (*from top to bottom*).

An authentic *laguiole* from Passion France
created together with Robert Beillonnet,
one of the best knife makers in France.
Photo: *Passion France*

Along with the *laguiole*, Opinel knives are
among France's most successful exports.
The cutting ability of the knife—developed
in 1890—is first-class.
Photo: *Opinel*

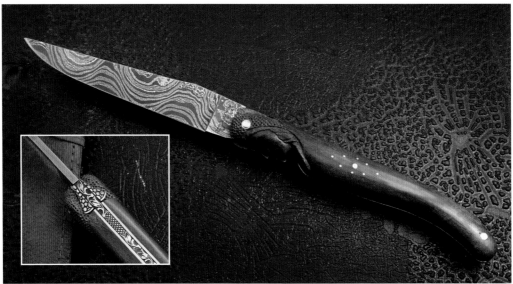

This *laguiole* was made by craftsman Pierre Martin for Laguiole en Aubrac. The fine
craftsmanship makes it a work of art.

and a sheep's-foot blade. For many years Otter has made the Mercator, a simple knife that has been available in almost identical form for more than 100 years. The almost indestructible steel version, usually painted black, has now been joined by versions with a brass or copper handle.

French Folding Knives

Typical of the French is their deep connection to the region in which they live and grew up. This regional sense of belonging is also visible in their knives. Even today there are easily fifty different types of folding knife in daily use: preparing *casse-croûte* (French for "lunch" or "snack"), and working in the garden, in the field and the pastures, in the coastal areas and at sea, and in the vineyards. The world-famous Opinel is joined by knives such as the Corsican Vendetta, the sailor's Montpellier, or the *poisson culot* (fresh fish).

Considered the most beautiful and most "French" knife is the Laguiole. This slender, characteristically formed knife from the heart of France is named for its place of origin—a village in Aubrac—and is known worldwide for its elegance. There are few who can escape its beauty. It is just as at home in the callused hands of a farmer as it is in the delicate fingers of a young woman. And when a few men get together for *casse-croûte* in France, someone first rummages about in his pockets and then talks. About what? About the Laguiole of course.

"With or without corkscrew" is the key question, which is followed by other essential questions. Should the handle be made of

TRIVIA: THE LAGUIOLE KNIFE: Elegant Lines

The history of the Laguiole goes back a good 150 years and begins in southwestern France. Laguiole—a small village on the volcanic high plateau of Massif-Central—is the birthplace and name-giver of the best-known French knife.

In addition to fixed, slender *capuchadou* knives, at the beginning of the nineteenth century the village smiths began making a simple folding knife used by the stockbreeders and farmers of the region for their work and for many day-to-day cutting tasks.

That is, until one of the village smiths decided to create something new: on the basis of a folding knife then in widespread use, the *yssingeaux*, he created a knife of his own. More delicately shaped, with a line falling gently to the handle end and equipped with a curved, Arab-inspired blade, it was soon the dominant knife in local trouser pockets. The designation Laguiole is not protected, which is why this type of knife is frequently copied.

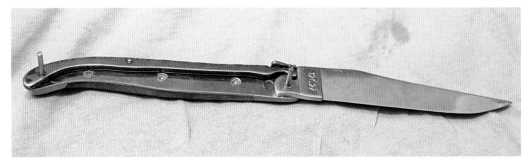

The special *laguiole* "Cran Forcé" locking mechanism can be seen on this knife. The back spring not only rests on the blade heel, also hooking it a little.

ethereal-smelling juniper wood or supple yellowish boxwood? Or instead horn—the traditional handle material—shimmering and hard? Does one want a blade of stainless steel or does one prefer a non-stainless carbon steel, whose patina will soon tell of the knife's everyday use?

Italian Folding Knives

Maniago is a small city in northern Italy with about 12,000 inhabitants and is the undisputed center of Italian knife production. It has been verified that the large-scale production of knives and other cutlery has been going on there since 1453. Today some of the best-known pocketknives and jackknives in the world come from manufacturers from Maniago.

About 180 miles farther south, near Florence, is the town Scarperia. There, too, the tradition of the knife trade can be traced back to the Middle Ages. Many historical pocketknife types are still produced by companies such as Coltellerie Berti (since 1895), the Coltellerie Consigli, and the Coltellerie Saladini. These include the Mozzetta, a knife without a point, or the Sardinian Pattada with its pointed, lead-shaped blade.

Spanish Folding Knives

La navaja means the pocketknife. With a blade length of 8 inches and more, even in former times the *navaja* must not have been all that suitable for carriage in trousers. These long blades were suitable for hot-blooded confrontations.

No specific blade shape was or is specified for the *navaja*. In addition to wide-bellied, slender, and almost triangular blades, as well as sage leaf–shaped and the currently popular curved, pointed, and thinly tapered blades, there are many other forms of blade. A noticeable thing about these models compared to modern knives is their moderate blade thickness, which rarely exceeds 0.08 to 0.11 inches.

They say that Sardinians "have the knife in their blood." The Pattada is a classic shepherd's knife (here an example from Vittorio Mura). It is one of the best-known types of Italian knife.

The Spanish term for folding knife is *navaja*, which ranges from huge (overall length up to 19.7 inches) to small and practical. Here is a selection from Pallarès Solsona.

The handle is often artfully decorated and usually has a pronounced bend. The butt is thinly tapered and can be bordered with metal or made completely of metal and riveted to the handle.

Catalan manufacturer Pallarès Solsona is known for particularly low-priced *navajas* that have a one-piece plastic handle. While they cost only a few Euros, they cut like the proverbial devil.

What this Spaniard is holding is not a sword but a traditional *navaja*. He is wearing his blanket around his waist like a belt with the knife stuck in it, clearly visible as a warning.

A special feature of original Spanish *navajas* is a locking mechanism called a *caracca*. The blade heel was toothed, so that a characteristic warning sound was made when the blade opened: "Now it's getting serious!" The mechanism also prevented the blade from suddenly snapping shut. *Navajas* were and are produced in Albacete, Seville, Toledo, Malaga, Mallorca, Madrid, Solsona, and other cities.

British Folding Knives

The first indications of knife making in Sheffield are found in taxation reports from 1297. London was initially also involved in the manufacture of knives in a big way. It was not until the seventeenth century that Sheffield took the top spot away from the English capital.

In the age of waterpower, Sheffield, with its many streams and the availability of coal and sandstone—suitable for the production of high-quality grinding stones—was in a privileged position. Soon many other industries (file makers and manufacturers of nails, buttons, and scissors) settled in the city. At the time, the entire city must have resembled a huge factory, whose individual departments were the city districts.

In the eighteenth century, Sheffield became the steel capital of the entire world. This was due not just to its good craftsmen. After the necessary iron ore was initially imported from Sweden, in the 1740s the English succeeded in developing cast steel, which qualitatively was unsurpassed.

Anyone who has read Mark Twain's
Huckleberry Finn probably remembers this
knife: a Barlow. This example is made by
Taylor's Eye Witness in Sheffield.

In the nineteenth century, Sheffield provided the whole world
with knives, and the US was one of its most important markets.
Americans eventually began making them on their own, as this
Barlow from Ka-Bar shows.

The demise of the knife industry in Sheffield had many reasons: first, important export markets broke away. America was the most important market for the knife makers of Sheffield, and special knives were even made for trade with Native Americans (references to "scalping knives" from Sheffield are found in writings from the 1830s). And even the "typically American" Barlow pocketknife, made world famous by Mark Twain's *Huckleberry Finn*, was originally a type of knife from Sheffield.

The Barlow is a folding work knife with one or two blades. Most of the twin-blade models have a longer clip point blade and a shorter pen blade. They were probably first produced in the seventeenth century. Characteristic features are the lengthened handle spine, giving the knife stability, and a teardrop-shaped handle.

At some point, manufacturers in the United States—thanks to the immigration of knife professionals from Solingen and Sheffield—began making their own knives. And in the two world wars, Sheffield—the center of the British arms industry—was almost completely destroyed and has never completely recovered. Today only a few manufacturers remain. The most important is the tradition-rich Sheffield company Taylor's Eve Eye Witness, which produces traditional pocketknives and cutlery.

American Folding Knives

There is a large market in the US for traditional folding knives. If one looks at the case of the product line of knife manufacturer W. R. Case, one can also understand why: this company alone offers dozens of different pocketknife models whose blade composition and handle shapes are historically verifiable. There are twin-blade trappers' knives used to skin muskrat; Texas Toothpicks, which are surely not used only as toothpicks; and canoe knives, whose handle shape is reminiscent of the canoes used by Native Americans. Almost every model is available with a wide variety of handle details.

The colors of the bone scales bore names such as Root Beer or Pocket Worn Harvest Orange. The latter was supposed to feel as if one had already carried the knife in one's pocket all year.

Among the best-known American classics is the Stockman, which almost every manufacturer has in its catalog. It was the classic folding work knife used by cowboys. The three-blade structure is typical, with a long clip point blade and a shorter but powerful sheep's-foot blade on one end and a spey blade on the opposite axis. The latter was used to castrate cattle, which now is no longer done this way. Having several blades is quite practical. If one is dull, one takes the

Traditional folding knives have a huge community of fans in the US. Here is a selection from Case. At the top and bottom of the photo are two examples of the Sway Back Jack, and between them are two Stockmans in different sizes.

TRIVIA: CONGRESS KNIFE: Six Blades for the President

American folding knives also come in finer versions. One such model is the six-blade Congress knife. American president Abraham Lincoln was carrying one such knife, with silver mounting and ivory scales—probably manufactured in Sheffield, England— on the night he was assassinated, together with a brown leather wallet, a white linen handkerchief with "A. Lincoln" embroidered in red, and a gold counterweight for his pocket watch. There was also one pair of gold-rimmed spectacles with sliding temples (one of the bows was mended with string), one pair of folding spectacles in a silver case, a watch fob of gold-bearing quartz, and eight newspaper clippings.

The blade of this mini *higonokami* is classically made with three layers (San Mai): the core with the cutting edge is made of highly hardened nonstainless carbon steel, while the two outer layers are low-alloy steel. Traditional bronze is used for the one-piece handle.

Relatives: an original Japanese *higonokami* with a large axis nut and, below it, a folding knife of similar design from Citadel.

next one—and for food preparation one can use another blade for "dirty" jobs.

Japanese Folding Knives

Japan is a land of special knives—especially cooking knives. When it comes to folding knives, *higonokami* is one of the best-known and homely representatives. The starting point for its development must have been a knife whose handle was probably engraved with the legend Higonokami (*Higo No Kami*). Kami is an aristocratic title that can be translated as lord or governor. Higo Province is now part of the Kumamoto Prefecture in southwestern Japan.

The Governor of Higo knife reached Miki, in the Hyogo Prefecture, at the end of the nineteenth century. Whether it looked like the *higonokami* we know today is uncertain. In Miki, there has been a knife-makers guild since 1899, and various members of the guild made the knife under the name "Hirata," named after a city district of Miki. In 1910, the term *higonokami* was protected as a trademark, and only members of the guild could so call their knives. Today there is just one remaining *higonokami* maker that can call on this guild tradition: Nagao from Miki.

Typically a *higonokami* has an engraved handle of curved brass to which the forged blade is attached by a large rivet, and into which it completely disappears. There is no spring and no lock. Instead, the blade has a simple lever with which it can more easily be opened and then folded into the handle.

For many decades the *higonokami* was Japan's most popular pocketknife and was a part of the basic equipment for Japanese men. In schools it was used in wood shop and to sharpen pencils, but in the 1960s, a new and very strict law was passed: henceforth, knives were not allowed in schools. The *higonokami* was also supplanted by more-modern pocketknives. A few small manufacturers, mainly micro-entities, still produce this type of knife.

The Best-Known Types

Folding knives are classified principally by their function: gentlemen's knives are stylish everyday accompaniments, while knives used in emergencies are rescue knives or tactical folders. Here you will discover the most-important classes of folding knives, their development histories, and their most important representatives.

Gentleman's Pocketknife

Finely made pocketknives with a discrete, stylish exterior are usually referred to as gentlemen's knives. The link between the functional cutting tool and the noblemen of the world is no coincidence. One or two generations ago, a pocketknife was part of almost every man's basic equipment. Since even a gentleman wanted to be prepared for the eventualities of everyday life, he of course carried a sharp blade. The times have changed, but it is still the carefully selected articles of daily use such as a fine leather wallet, a precise pen, or even an elegant-yet-functional knife that make the difference between normal and stylish.

If you are not sure whether your knife belongs in the category of gentleman's knife, then put yourself in the following situation: you are a guest at an elegant party and you notice that the hostess is struggling with a stubborn package. You go over to her, reach into your pocket, and pass the hostess your pocketknife. If she accepts your knife, uses it, and returns it, possibly with the comment that it is a lovely pocketknife, you have made the right knife selection.

If you receive a distraught look and after the episode receive no further invitations, it might be another type of knife (see "Tactical Folding Knives" at the end of the chapter).

Folding Hunting Knives

Among the typical tasks after a successful kill is gutting the animal that has been brought down: hunter's parlance for removing the organs and intestines from the animal as quickly as possible to keep the meat hygienic for later consumption. This is done by opening the abdominal and chest areas and removing the intestines through

Fine gentlemen's knives are clearly a strength of traditional Japanese manufacturer Moki.

TRIVIA: EDC AND UTILITY KNIFE: Simply Always There

The abbreviation EDC stands for Every Day Carry. It refers to a knife designed to be well suited to everyday cutting tasks. It is also important that an EDC knife be comfortable to carry. An EDC can thus be a gentleman's knife just as well as a tactical folder—only the demands are different. Other items of everyday equipment are often also grouped under EDC, from a wallet to a flashlight.

A utility knife is a knife that first and foremost is functional, and that means that it is first of all good for cutting. Also important is a high level of operating safety and a comfortable handle.

Four practical and elegant everyday companions as made by Fantoni, Victorinox, Nilte, and Spyderco (*from top to bottom*).

the anus. To do this one needs a sharp and controllable blade.

For this reason a folding hunting knife is standard equipment for many hunters. Thanks to their relatively compact dimensions, they fit into a pocket in the trousers or jacket and are always accessible when needed. The sharp blade is safely stowed in the handle. It is often said, "The more experienced the hunter, the shorter the blade." If one knows what one is doing, then one can cope with a 3-inch blade when taking care of native wildlife.

Nevertheless, the blades are often somewhat longer. Should the hunter ever find himself in a situation in which a wounded animal must be stabbed to death because a firearm cannot be used for whatever reason, then a longer blade is absolutely necessary.

In addition to a drop point universal blade, most multipart folding hunting knives also have a gutting blade: it is curved inward and, instead of a normal point, often has a rounded, spherical point. It is used to make an upward cut into the abdominal cavity without running the danger of inadvertently puncturing the internal organs. A saw is also practical, since sticks cut to a precise length are very useful when hunting, such as for a hiking aid.

Rescue Knives

Emergency care in Germany is good. After the command center receives an emergency call via telephone number 112, it transmits the information to the police, fire department, or rescue service, and help arrives quickly. Relatively quickly, since ten or even twenty minutes from the receipt of the call by the command center can be too long: for example, if after an accident the driver of an automobile cannot get out because he cannot reach the seat belt release or the door is jammed.

More and more manufacturers are making specialized tool knives equipped with belt cutters and glass breakers. The belt-cutting blades are often serrated to cut through tough fabrics. For safety their point is rounded.

Window breakers should taper and be made of hardened steel or tungsten carbide. They are used to strike the corners of safety glass panels, offering the best chance of success. To expand the usage spectrum—for opening and cutting dressing material, cutting off clothing, or cutting rope—a separate blade makes sense.

Some manufacturers, such as Victorinox of Switzerland, go even further. The company's RescueTool, designed for professional firefighters, is also equipped with a belt pouch, fluorescent handle scales, a lever blade, and a disc saw for cutting through laminated glass. It is truly sufficient to break into any vehicle.

The Buck 110—seen here is a special version with oak handle scales and a blade made of 5160 carbon steel—is probably the best-known folding knife in the world.

From its window breaker to its belt-cutting blade to its saw for cutting through laminated glass, the Victorinox RescueTool has everything one might need.

Sal Glesser, owner of Spyderco, is himself an enthusiastic sailor, and the Tusk is his idea of a perfect sailing knife. Nitrogen-alloyed LC200N special steel, which is very rust resistant, is used for the blade. The blade and the marlinspike lock.

Behind the Ulize, which German knifemaker Uli Hennicke designed for Spyderco, are the requirements of a long-serving SEK official: it is designed for police searches, for use in rescuing and freeing persons, for capturing injured animals, and more.

Maritime Folding Knife

What one needs onboard a sailing ship is an appropriate knife; there is always a rope or cable to cut, a tarpaulin to cut into, or a knot to loosen. That is when the maritime knife comes to the fore.

It has a typical blade shape: on most models the cutting edge is straight as a die and ends—as the blade spine drops off quite steeply to the cutting edge—less in a point than in a sharp corner. This allows very precise work to be carried out. Another reason for the absence of a point is increased safety when using the knife.

The straight cutting edge enables especially forceful and controlled cuts on hanging or tensioned ropes. If very heavy cable must be cut, one places the blade on it with the edge facing down and drives it through the cable with blows from a mallet. The blade and the rivet connection must of course be sufficiently strong.

Many knives, such as the Bundeswehr's shipboard knife, have a so-called marlinspike. This is a sturdy, rounded metal mandrel with which one can break ropes down into individual strands (so-called splaying) and loosen stuck knots. Another typical feature of maritime knives is an eye or handle to attach the knife to the wearer's clothing.

Tactical Folding Knives

The term "tactical folder" has become an integral part of the knife scene. But what exactly is a tactical folding knife? Is the Spanish *navaja*—with its long blade—which was also carried for self-defense, tactical? Is a Mercator knife, invented in the second half of the nineteenth century and used by soldiers of the Prussian army, a tactical folder?

In a way, yes—if by a tactical folding knife one means that a knife useful in everyday use becomes a survival knife if required and, in an emergency, can be used for self-defense.

Among the first manufacturers to produce tactical folding knives was the American company Al Mar. The Eagle was an elegant, slender, and all the same sturdy folding knife. The SERE (Survival, Evasion, Resistance, Escape), which was soon developed from it, was and is an almost indestructible monster of a knife that because of its relative compactness (compared to a fixed combat knife) can always be at hand and is intended to be a reliable tool and weapon for soldiers in an emergency.

TRIVIA: TACTICAL FOLDING KNIFE: The Tactical Folder

It was American knife maker Bob Terzuola who around 1990 coined the term "tactical folder" and claimed it for himself. Together with other knife makers such as Ernest Emerson, he specialized in folding knives whose blade can be made ready for action quickly and is strong enough to survive even improper use, which can happen any time when in action.

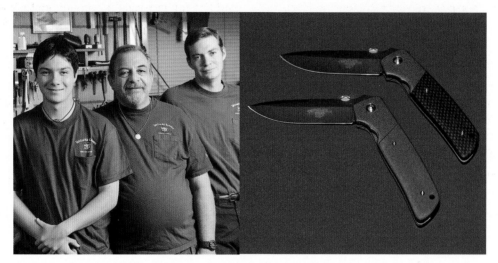

American knifemaker Bob Terzuola (here with his sons in the workshop) is a bedrock of the tactical-knife scene. He is regarded as the inventor of the term "tactical folder."

Ernest Emerson set the standard for tactical knives with the CQC-7. *Emerson*

Chapter Summary

Folding knives are not a recent invention: the oldest known folding knife is about 2,500 years old. The biggest advantage of a folding knife compared to a fixed knife is its compactness: the sharp and pointed blade can be almost as long as the handle and disappears when it is not needed.

The simplest folding knife consists of just a blade, an axial pin, and a handle with recess. Pocketknives whose blade is held in position by a back spring first appeared about 250 years ago—when spring steel first became widely available.

Folding knives whose extended blades are reliably locked in position are particularly safe to use. Numerous mechanisms have been developed for this purpose. Among the best known are the locking collar (Opinel), the back lock (as on the Buck 110), the liner lock (for example, the M Series by CRKT), and the frame lock (Chris Reeve Sebenza).

In many nations of this world, very special types of knives have developed over the centuries and are now considered characteristic of their land of origin. These include the world-famous Swiss Army Knife and the folding-lever automatic knife from Germany, the Laguiole from France, the clicking *navaja* from Spain, the cowboy folding knife from the US, and the Japanese *higonokami*.

Among the best-known folding knives are fine gentlemen's knives, distinguished by their elegant optics and frequently by special materials and elaborately worked details. In contrast, the most-important features of so-called tactical folding knives are quick usability of the blade and especially solid construction.

A lever lock switchblade with typical folding lever, here with a Damasteel blade made by Hubertus of Solingen.

Chapter 5.
Straight Razors:
Smooth with Style

James Bond did not exactly have it easy in the movie *Skyfall*: first he was shot by his female colleague Eve Moneypenny and was subsequently declared dead. Later he was also lathered—in the truest sense of the word—by Moneypenny, since when she gave Bond important information, he was just preparing to give himself a close shave. Moneypenny then took matters into her own hands—in the classic style, with a straight razor.

Would James put his life in her hands again? He did, because "sometimes the old-fashioned way is still the best." Eve and James, wearing only a towel, agreed and became closer than ever before.

It is film appearances such as this one, or the bloody opening sequence from *Gangs of New York* with Leonardo DiCaprio and Daniel Day-Lewis, that brought the straight razor into the consciousness of a new generation. Incidentally, after the described James Bond movie scene, razor manufacturers quadrupled their sales.

The straight razor is a part of cutting-tool culture. Initially the razor consisted of sharp-edged, flaked obsidian, then later of copper, bronze, and even gold, and still later of iron

and steel. Straight razors with a quality of steel resembling that of today first became known in the middle of the eighteenth century.

In the past, shaving with a straight razor was standard practice, since the safety razor was not developed until the beginning of the twentieth century. Today, shaving with the blade is a skill in which many men are again showing an interest.

Almost every man has wondered what shaving with a blade feels like, and if it really is a good idea to cut the stubble from the throat with an extremely sharp blade.

Of course it is a good idea! A straight razor is the symbol for sharpness at the highest level, and it is a purchase for life. This puts into perspective the purchase price, which for entry-level straight razors is in the area of fifty dollars but, depending on the model, can be several times that amount. Anyone without a razor in his collection is missing something.

Once one has mastered the blade, shaving can become a trouble-free and relaxing matter. A sharp blade shaves even more smoothly than five blades, which must be "behind bars." And whoever celebrates his

Straight-Razor Types and Edges

Straight-Razor Grind
Cross Sections

Typical Blade Points

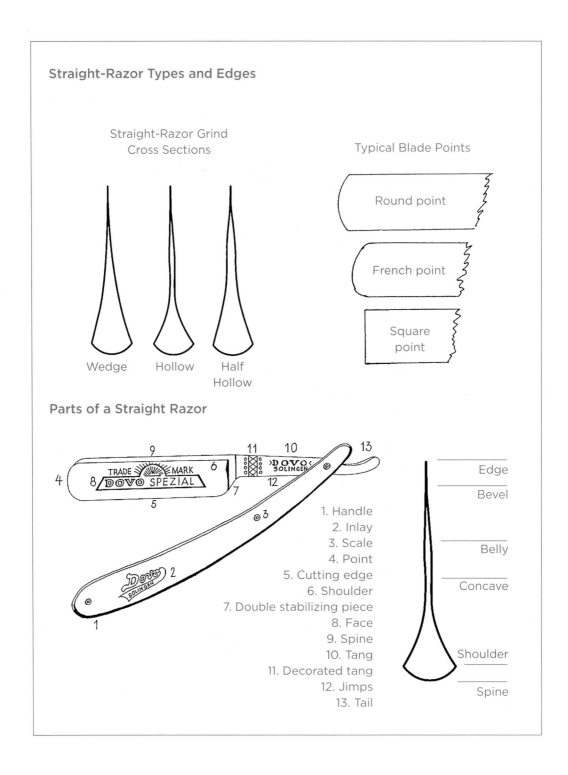

Wedge   Hollow   Half
Hollow

Round point

French point

Square
point

Parts of a Straight Razor

TRADE MARK
DOVO SPEZIAL

DOVO
SOLINGEN

Dovo
SOLINGEN

1. Handle
2. Inlay
3. Scale
4. Point
5. Cutting edge
6. Shoulder
7. Double stabilizing piece
8. Face
9. Spine
10. Tang
11. Decorated tang
12. Jimps
13. Tail

Edge

Bevel

Belly

Concave

Shoulder

Spine

shave with everything that goes with it—with hot towels in preparation, good-smelling shaving cream, and a nice aftershave—can forget about the next wellness vacation.

Straight-Razor Shapes and Grind Types

The variety of straight-razor edge types and blade shapes has diminished in the past decades. While the so-called Henckel scale still has fourteen increments of hollow grind, today there are five primary types: coarse, half hollow, three-quarters hollow and full hollow, and less commonly extra hollow.

With the coarse grind, the blade has almost a wedge shape, while in the case of full and extra-hollow grinds the blades are concave from just beneath the blade spine, with large parts of the blade being very thin.

The hollower the blade, the more flexible it is, and the more feedback one receives while shaving—both tactually and acoustically. Then the connoisseurs say the razor is singing. In the truest sense of the word, the blade must be razor sharp over the entire edge.

A hollow-ground straight razor in the traditional Solingen style is not ground to zero in one go; instead, it has two adjoining, differently pronounced concave edges. In the transition area between the two hollow grinds is the "wall." This is a slight reinforcement of the blade over its entire length. It gives the cutting facet necessary support and makes it possible for a razor to be repeatedly ground thin for many years. The facet itself must be so thin that

it bows when placed on its side on a nail (the proverbial thumbnail test).

The width of the blade is specified in increments of an eighth of an inch. Typical widths are between 3/8 and 7/9 of an inch. Straight razors with the last-named width are referred to as swords. The narrower the blade, the less of the face it hides, which is often recommended as helpful when working around contours. Half- to full-hollow razors in widths of 4/8 and 5/8 of an inch are considered all-rounders.

In conclusion, one differentiates between round, spike, and French or Spanish point. The edged point demands particular caution, since it is easier to cut oneself with it, although this point allows one to shave the contours of the face precisely.

Steel for Straight Razors

A razor with a non-stainless-steel blade is called a "straight razor with normal steel." A popular steel alloy is the wear-resistant and yet fine-grained 1.2210, which is called "silver steel." The term comes from tool-making, where it refers to the shiny drawn material with a high carbon content. The name therefore has nothing to do with silver; rather, it is a reference to the shiny surface of the drawn steel. Instead of silver, 1.2210 contains 1.2 percent carbon and about 0.7 percent chromium, which raises wear resistance. The silver steel is hardened to 59 to 72 HRC (Hardness Rockwell C).

Corrosion-resistant 1.4034 "standard steel" from Solingen, or its 1.4037 variant with increased carbon content of 0.6 to

0.7 percent, is also sometimes used. It is somewhat easier to care for and achieves hardness from 57 to a maximum of 60 HRC.

Experienced users report that when shaving, there are almost no differences between the two types of steel. Corrosion-resistant straight razors come at the cost of rather more effort in stropping (freshening the cutting edge with the help of a razor strop).

Caring for the Straight Razor

After use, a straight razor is rinsed with clean water and carefully dried. This should be done carefully because the cutting edge is very sensitive, and even contact with cotton fibers can result in loss of sharpness.

Contact between the cutting edge and anything harder than a human hair should absolutely be avoided. Use caution when opening and closing the razor, since the handle scales can warp! Common tests to check sharpness, such as cutting paper, also lead to dulling. And of course one should not try to catch a razor that slips from the hand, or from the edge of the wash basin. Better a professional sharpening than a deep cut!

Blades made of nonrustproof steel are treated with a little oil if they are to be stored for longer periods. Camellia oil is recommended.

Straight-Razor Accessories

In addition to the straight razor, one needs at least one razor strop (more on sharpening straight razors in chapter 12). Some users claim that they can maintain the sharpness of their straight razor only by using leather. The fact is that stropping is indispensable; one has to master it. Professionals also provide sharpening.

Anyone who wants to sharpen their straight razor or refurbish a flea market find needs whetstones. Japanese waterstones, Arkansas whetstones, and Belgian Blue whetstones have all proven effective.

To make shaving as easy and comfortable as possible, one should invest in a good shaving brush. One needs shaving soap or cream and a soap dish for whisking the foam. A styptic pencil stops minor bleeding.

Chapter Summary

The classic straight razor is a symbol for sharpness at the highest level. Traditional manufacturers make high-quality and fascinatingly beautiful razors that do well in any collection, although they are actually much too good to merely look at. One can shave very thoroughly and comfortably with classic straight razors, provided one masters their care and basic shaving strokes—and one can learn these relatively easily.

TRIVIA: STRAIGHT RAZOR: Etiquette

▸ A straight razor is always passed to another closed.
▸ When closing, carefully guide the blade between the scales. Do not casually snap it closed like a pocketknife.
▸ Do not test sharpness with a finger or thumb.
▸ After shaving, carefully clean and dry the razor.
▸ Between shaving and stropping, give the edge about a day to recover.

An archaic fixed razor (*far left*) from Japan (Kamisori), and beside it Solingen blades from traditional manufacturers Dovo; Böker; Golddachs, Giesen & Forsthoff; Wacker; and Puma.

TRIVIA: MANUFACTURE: How a Straight Razor Is Made

▶ Altogether, the making of a straight razor like those made by Dovo in Solingen consists of about eighty work steps. Here are the most important.

▶ The so-called slugs are cut from steel bands. These are pieces of metal that are somewhat longer and wider than the eventual blades.

▶ These slugs are heated to about 2,010°F and in a Solingen drop forge are pounded into shapes—so-called dies—by a very heavy hammer. The spine, blade, and tang receive their later contour and cross section. The shaping in the closed drop forge is precise to within a few tenths of a millimeter.

▶ During the deburring process, excess metal is removed from the "wing." The shape of the straight razor blade is already clearly visible.

▶ Then the tang is milled or ground to size, the hole to accept the rivet is drilled, and, if necessary, the future trademark is applied on the tang.

▶ The blanks are subsequently hardened in a hardening plant, and depending on the alloy, each is heated to 1,490 to 1,900°F in a lead bath. The blades are first covered with graphite dust to prevent the lead from sticking. The subsequent quenching takes place in hardening oil or, in the case of stainless steel, air.

▶ After the blades are cleaned, they are annealed at about 390°F. This reduces the internal tensions in the steel microstructure created by the heating process. The steel loses some of its hardness but becomes tougher.

▶ Tempering of the blades is subsequently done manually by eye with the hammer.

▶ The quenched and tempered blades subsequently receive their hollow grinding, here called hollow. An experienced grinder (the hollow grinder previously underwent master training) pushes them between two rotating circular grindstones. Their radius determines the degree of hollow. Different grindstones of ever-finer grit are used. The spine and the tang are also cleanly ground.

▶ The current IHK professional title for the straight-razor grinder is toolmaker, specialization instrumentation technology. In vocational training it is cutting-tool mechanic.

▶ The blades are then fine-ground on small felt or leather (walrus neck leather) wheels and receive their finish. The wheels are rubbed with a mixture of glue and corundum. A high concentration is always necessary so that the entire length of the cutting edge becomes as thin as a razor blade. The material must not be overheated during this process so that it retains its hardness and cutting properties.

▶ The blades then usually undergo laser engraving, and some are gold-plated (damascening), which is applied electrolytically.

▶ Then the handle scales are fitted. The blade is held in place between the scales by a German silver pin. Under no circumstances can the cutting edge touch the handle; otherwise it will be damaged.

▶ The blade receives its ultimate razor sharpness by means of a slightly concave dish grinding wheel, bank grinding stones, and leather. The goal is an edge polished to nothing with maximum fineness.

▶ Sharpness is checked with a hair, which must "leap over the blade" at the slightest touch. Other sharpness tests, such as cutting paper, are completely unsuited for especially finely ground straight-razor blades.

▶ Polishing work on the handle, as well as lubricating, cleaning, and packing in cartons, completes the work.

Chapter 6. Multitools: Multifunctional Heavyweights

The invention of the modern multitool in pliers form is inseparably linked with Tim Leatherman, whose name became synonymous with the multitool. In the 1970s, Tim traveled through Europe and the Near East with his wife, and he frequently had problems with his temperamental automobile but had no suitable tools on hand. For the most part he got by with the aid of a traditional Boy Scout folding knife, but it had no pliers.

In a hotel room in Teheran, the trained mechanical engineer made the first cardboard templates for a compact, versatile tool. Back home, he fiddled about with his brother-in-law until he was able to present a multifunction tool with a folding pliers head and other tools, such as a blade, can opener, and screwdriver.

In 1980, Tim Leatherman patented (US Patent 4238862) his Mr. Crunch, as he named the tool. Even the *New York Times* reported on the tool, and Leatherman assumed that someone would purchase the patent from him for millions of dollars, but no one was interested in his invention.

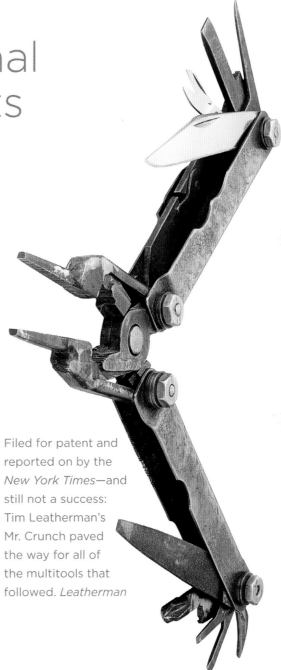

Filed for patent and reported on by the *New York Times*—and still not a success: Tim Leatherman's Mr. Crunch paved the way for all of the multitools that followed. *Leatherman*

The expected success and associated profits did not materialize; Mr. Crunch probably looked too crude and unusual. Not until 1983, with the introduction of the PST (Personal Survival Tool), did Leatherman's unbroken run of success begin. As its central component, the PST had a regular folding combination pliers head, and it was also equipped with a blade, metal file, and saw, and the most-common screwdrivers. Legend has it that Leatherman offered his design to knife maker Gerber, but Gerber turned him down.

The first PST, with serial number 001, was bought by the German collector Wolf Schulz-Tattenpach, who met Tim Leatherman at a knife show in Eugene, Oregon, in 1983. Wolf Schulz-Tattenpach, who remains friends with Leatherman to this day, told the story:

Tim Leatherman approached us and invited my business partner Peter and me to join him at his table. Tim wanted to find out which components he should use to equip his PST. His table was covered with pliers heads, blades, screwdrivers, and saws. And so I put the tool together in a way I thought made sense. Soon afterward he asked Peter for his opinion, and he decided on exactly the same combination of tools. Tim was completely astonished and asked us if we thought such a tool would be a success. What a question! I gave him my visitor's card and ordered the first Personal Survival Tool, which I received on May 7, 1983.

Since that day more than 150 million Leatherman tools have been sold. But Leatherman was not the first to come up with the idea of a pliers multitool—far from it.

Forerunner of the Multitool

Much older than Leatherman & Company is a mechanic's tool with a combination pliers head bearing the name E. Behrman L'Électric. This robust pliers knife is made of non-rustproof carbon steel and was produced in France. Not much is known about it, but it is believed to have been used by electricians in Paris between the First and Second World Wars. At first the multifunction tool was equipped with three tool blades: one blade was 2.7 inches long and 0.09 inches thick, the second was a screwdriver with a wire stripper, and the third was probably a metal file (this blade has broken off the illustrated example). Each blade was held in position by its own firm back spring.

The pliers head with wire cutter is 1.2 inches long. Half of the head is an integral part of the lower outer board and thus immovable. A bolt with a nut forms the hinge and joins one half of the head with the movable second half, which turns into a shank limb. With the gripping surfaces lying on top of each other, this shank limb rests on the side of the handle and can be securely locked with a bracket. This French multifunction tool is 5.3 inches long, weighs about 6.7 ounces, and after all these years is still absolutely usable. A fantastic piece.

One of the rarer knives with multifunction is the PLI-R-NIF, which was patented by Christian Heilrath (from Sacramento, California) on May 23, 1905. The mechanism

The Heilrath PLI-R-NIF was one of the world's first multitools. It was patented in 1905.

The E. Behrman L'Électric was made in France and was used mainly by electricians between the First and Second World Wars.

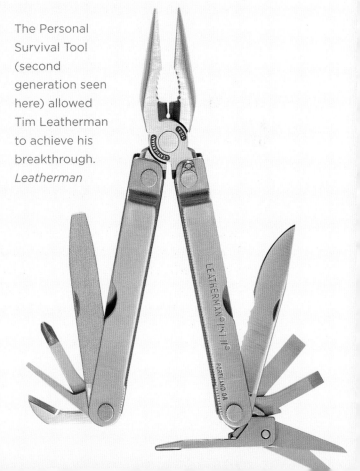

The Personal Survival Tool (second generation seen here) allowed Tim Leatherman to achieve his breakthrough. *Leatherman*

The Super Tool 300 by
Leatherman is one of the
heaviest and most powerful tools
on the market. This burnished
EOD version has special tools
for military demolition experts.
Leatherman

The Leatherman Crunch has an
effective vice grip, and the SOG
Powerlock has a gear drive. The
SwissTool Spirit is particularly
ergonomically shaped.

of the Heilrath tool is completely simple: basically the tool knife consists of four plates. Two of them each form a unit and the frame for a tool blade.

The lower end of the two upper plates accommodates a universal blade with a length of 2.4 inches and a maximum thickness of 0.09 inches. This blade does not lock but is held in place in the open or folded position by a sturdy back spring. The PLI-R-NIF's second tool is a slot screwdriver, but many models also have an awl. These tools are between the lower two plates. The two back springs extend upward, 1 inch above the plates, and are formed into pliers halves. A 0.2-inch nut forms the pliers pivot and joins the tool elements. With an overall length of 4.3 inches and a weight of just 2.7 ounces, the Heilrath tool is a light helper in many situations—and it has also become a sought-after collectors item.

Modern Multitools

Claw multitools were and are produced by companies such as SOG, Gerber, Buck, Victorinox, and Kershaw. The American company SOG Specialty Knives and Tools, founded in 1986, put its first multitool on the market in 1990. In form and design, with its external pliers head the so-called Tool Clip resembled the old French L'Électric tool. For many years it was made (also in a smaller version) in Seki, Japan's number one blade city. Unfortunately production was stopped. In 1995, SOG mastermind Spencer Frazer introduced the compound leverage system: a gear drive

for improved transmission of force to the pliers shanks.

The first tool from Gerber Legendary Blades appeared in 1992. For its time, the Multi-Plier was a good tool with a folding pliers head. Several blades and screwdrivers were accommodated in the handle halves. The first Gerber multitool had no locking system. This was first introduced some years later, and the tool was simultaneously renamed the Multi-Lock Tool. The tools from this series were later again called Multi-Plier and also had a tool lock, which by now has become standard.

The Swiss Victorinox company has had multifunction pocket tools in its catalog since it was founded in 1891. In the beginning they were Swiss-made soldiers' knives, but it would be 106 years before the company added a pliers multitool to its catalog. But when the SwissTool was unveiled in 1997, there was great excitement: what distinguishes this heavy multitool is its solid workmanship, locks for all of its tools, and the accessibility of all tools with the pliers head folded. The SwissTool is still one of the best multitools on the market.

The Victorinox SwissTool Spirit is the smaller brother of the SwissTool. The individual tools are somewhat shorter in comparison, but despite this they are very robust and durable. The Spirit has outstanding ergonomics thanks to its curved handle halves. With this piece of Swiss precision work at one's side, one is on the safe side in everyday and professional life, and in the outdoors. With the hard-chromed metal file one can even break open padlocks. And the combi pliers' cutting inserts make short work even of steel wire.

Chapter Summary

We have Tim Leatherman's car trouble during a trip to Europe in the 1970s to thank for the multitool we know today. Thank you Fiat! Since then, Leatherman has stood for multifunctionality in pocket format.

But Leatherman was not the first to invent a multifunctional pliers tool; there was a similar tool, the Military Wire Cutter Knife, around 1900. Among the most important modern manufacturers in addition to Leatherman are SOG, Gerber, Buck, Kershaw, and particularly Victorinox.

TRIVIA: MULTITOOLS: On a Secret Mission

Leatherman was not the first to bring a pliers multitool to market maturity. Clearly older than Leatherman & Co. is the Military Wire Cutter Knife by Joseph Rogers & Sons from Sheffield, England, which was patented in 1900 and produced until after the First World War. It had a wire cutter above the handle and two blades. This sturdy multitool was also used in the Second World War, but in modified form. In addition to the blade, the SOE/OSS Escape Knife housed in its handle three saw blades and a can opener, and in the end of the handle a screwdriver. SOE stood for Special Operations Executive, a British special intelligence service unit. OSS is the shortened form of the American Office of Strategic Services. The escape device was thus top secret.

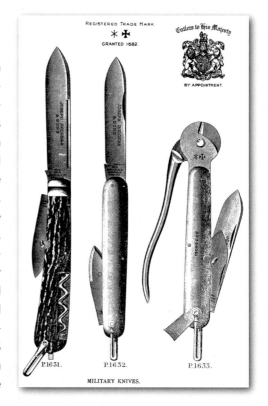

Old school: in the past there was no other choice but to take along one's tools individually.

On the SwissTool Spirit, the file is equipped with different chopping surfaces and a metal saw. The Leatherman Super Tool 300 accepts different saw blade inserts.

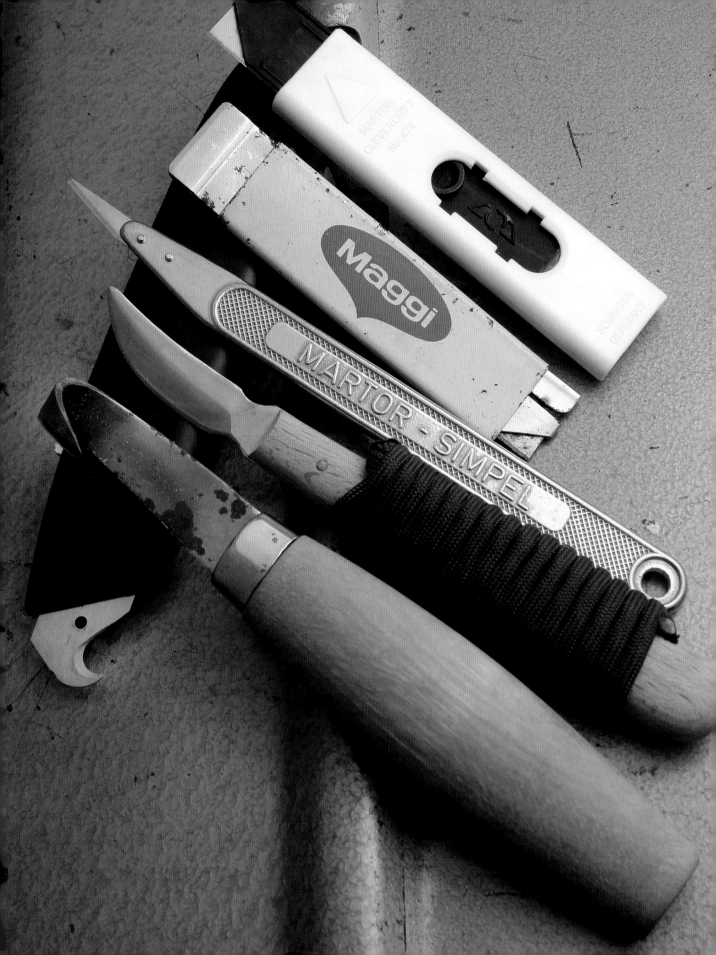

Chapter 7. Special Knives: The Specialists

Most users of hobby knives value those cutting tools suitable for a multitude of tasks. To professional users who find themselves confronted with recurring, special cutting tasks, it is different: someone who cuts foil or cardboard packaging all day only makes it unnecessarily hard on himself by using an outdoor knife.

Professionally, it makes sense to use cutting tools designed for a specific purpose. This is the domain of the special knife. Here is a selection of widely used, interesting, and unusual models.

Agricultural Knives

The age of the hunter-gatherer was followed by a more settled lifestyle, and with it farming. Among the most important farming tools were the hoe, plow, and scythe. While they were cutting tools, they were not knives.

There are a number of agricultural knives that were and are used for harvesting and for cutting and grafting plants, including sickles, as well as salad, budding, and pruning knives.

Sickles

Sickles appeared during the Bronze Age and were used for cutting grasses and wild grains. Their typical feature has remained the same for centuries: a tapering curved blade with a handle. The sickle differs from the scythe in its overall smaller blade and shorter handle.

Farmers' and Vintners' Knives

These knives are cutting and chopping tools used by farmers and vintners and are usually curved like sickles. They serve as universal tools for cutting, chopping, and lopping. Their typical shape consists of a handle from which a broad blade sticks straight out. Not until the last third does the blade curve, while the spine drops away in a crescent shape to the point. It thus resembles a raptor's beak. Folding pruning knives used for pulling cuts are very popular among hobby gardeners and professional users in nurseries and fruit orchards.

Salad Knives

Salad knives are used for harvesting lettuce. For this purpose their blade is offset to the side from the handle. This creates the nec-

The offset handle of the salad knife makes possible cuts just above the ground.

essary freedom to cut heads of lettuce just above the ground.

Garden Knives

Plants such as fruit trees or roses are cut and grafted so that they can thrive and be productive (through grafting, one passes the qualities of a parent plant to another plant part, so-called cultivation).

Two plants are combined through certain techniques. Thus, an apple tree that does well in existing soil conditions but bears sour and small apples can become a tree that is still firmly rooted, but whose apples really taste good.

Since this work often involves making hundreds of controlled, clean cuts every day, a good knife is indispensable; only a clean cut spares the plant and is suitable. After all, a surgeon also works with only the sharpest blades. Fine-grained steel is primarily used, frequently of nonstainless alloys. The cutting

angle is as small as possible so that the blade is as sharp as needed. The grip must always be sure and comfortable and rest comfortably in the hand.

Pruning Knives

Pruning knives are relatively long and have a sturdy, sharply curved blade. If something must be pruned they are the method of choice. The shape of the blade, with its upward-curving end, is determined by the shape of the handle. This allows the knife to rest surely in the hand during pulling cuts, for which it is designed. The normal pruning knife is used for pruning to trim the cut margin, to remove canker, and to cut off vertically growing water sprouts. It is also well suited for harvesting in herb gardens. Grafting knives are only slightly curved and have a narrower blade.

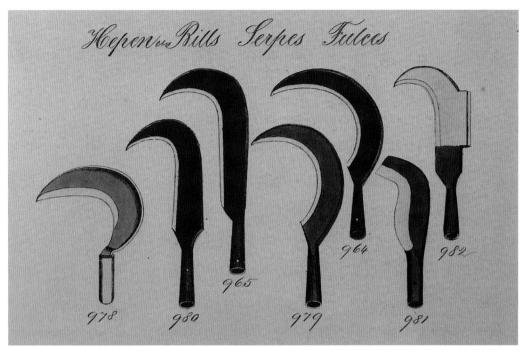

Models 980 and 965 show the classic gardener's and vintner's knife shape with a wide blade, the last third of which forms a curved point. This extract is from a Wolff pattern book (ca. 1850).

Victorinox combines bright colors with well-designed and sharpened florist knives. *Victorinox*

The pruning knife (here from Tina) is used for many jobs: pruning, trimming cuts, and more.

The saddler's hand knife is a versatile tool for leatherworking craftsmen.

A short blade enables the user to work forcefully but controlled. The blade on this shoemaker's knife from Tina is adjustable.

A fixed-blade linoleum knife with a second cutting edge on the spine.

Carving knives usually have short blades shaped to suit their intended use. At the top is a splint or chopping knife for hollowing.

Grafting Knives

Grafting blades are better suited for grafting many plants. Flower knives for florists also often have a straight sheep's-foot blade.

Grafting knives have either a specially formed—protruding and thinned—blade spine or an additional tool blade of brass or horn. These are used to lift and turn the bark without damage during grafting—another grafting technique.

Leather Knives

Leather was one of humanity's earliest raw materials. Today as then, it is made from the skins and hides of animals. The associated trades are tanner and leatherworker. Leather knives were and are also used by shoemakers and upholsterers.

Half-Moon Leather-Cutting Knife

The knife most commonly used by leatherworking tradesmen is semicircular or half-moon shaped. The edge is found along the entire curvature. The half-moon knife is used to cut and divide the finished skins, with the leatherworker moving the knife away from himself.

Pointed Saddler's Knife

The saddler's primary task is to make equipment—mainly of leather—for handling animals: bridles, belts, straps, and saddles. The tradesman needs a variety of different tools, including this pointed, almost triangular-shaped knife with a convex edge.

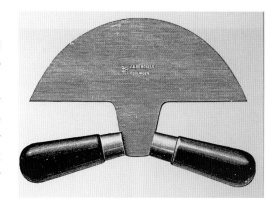

The half-moon knife (here with double handle, ca. 1905) is sharpened along the entire curvature.

Saddler's Hand Knife

A wide variety of knives are used for cutting workpieces from leather: half- and quarter-moon knives and hand knives with a variety of blade shapes. The main task of the hand knife is to "be quickly at hand." They are suitable for every possible type of job.

Shoemaker's Knife

A typical tool of this type has a slender, slightly bulbous blade. On the illustrated example (*left*), the blade length can be set. To do this, one opens a metal plate on the left side of the handle with five connectors that engage an element positioned on the side of the blade at the very end.

Leather and Linoleum Knife

Knives with sickle-shaped blades are also used for pulling cuts in leather or linoleum.

The pointed tip and inward-curved blade can be controlled and used effectively. On the spine of the model shown there is also a hook-shaped hollow-ground cutting edge.

Wood-Carving Knives

Carving involves shaping wood with a sharp blade. Short blades enable particularly forceful yet controlled use. A good hand position is important. Chisels are the primary tools for wood sculpture. They are not knives in the actual sense.

Wood-Carving and Chip-Carving Knives

In chip carving, one draws a design on wood and subsequently cuts it out with a sharp chip-carving knife. To do this, one needs a precisely sharpened and usually also very short blade.

Chisel Knife

Chisel knives are specially adapted to meet the needs of (wood) craftsmen and are used for coarse work such as cutting, chiseling, and sculpting. Knives of this type have two cutting areas: a straight main edge and a sharp ground chisel tip. Often these knives are so sturdy that they can be driven into wood with a carver's mallet.

Bookbinder Knives

For the handcrafted production of books and the restoration of old and, in some cases, valuable books and booklets, one needs sharp blades.

Bookbinder Knife

Bookbinder knives are so designed that they can be used to accurately cut almost any kind of paper. The book pages still connected after the binding process must be separated cleanly. For this, one needs a finely sharpened blade and a very manageable handle.

Edging Knives

Edging knives are used for edging, or thinning work on leather. They are also used on vellum and paper, but their edges must be finely thinned.

Replaceable-Blade Knives

The craft knifes of the past were often so solid and suitable that they could be used for an entire working life of at least many years. Of course they had to be cared for and sharpened.

But as the working world changed, especially after the Second World War, other requirements came to the foreground:

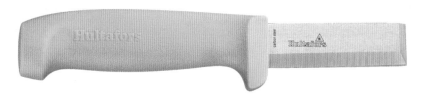

A very sturdy chisel knife from Hultafors. *Hultafors*

The bookbinder knife from Victorinox of Switzerland is very finely ground: directly above the cutting bevel it is just 0.25 mm thick.

Martor has created craftsmen's and safety knives with an excellent reputation. At the top is a deburring and graphic designer's knife for fine cuts.

cutting tasks in industrial operations were much more varied than before. There was no longer time for time-consuming care. Manufacturers therefore increasingly turned to special knives designed according to the "Gillette razor principle."

The blades of these models consisted of cheap steel strip rarely more than 0.09 inches thick, and as soon as they became too dull they were simply removed and replaced with a new blade. This was also made possible by the development of locking systems that could be used reliably, as well as quickly and comfortably.

Safety Knives

On early replaceable-blade knives, the blades, with their sharp blades, corners, and edges, often projected from the blade permanently. Those who did not exercise caution could quickly injure themselves. This resulted in the development of special safety knives. Martor of Solingen made a special name for itself in this field with its Secumax, Secupro, and Secunorm model lines.

The only knife that is really safe is one whose blade disappears into the handle as soon as it is not being used. To achieve this, the blades of Martor knives are spring-loaded and can be pushed out of the handle only against the pressure of the spring. They do not lock: as soon as the forward push ends, the blade slides completely back into the handle. On a fully automatic retraction (another variant), the blade is pulled back into the handle as soon as cutting pressure

on the base drops—including in the case of an accidental slip.

Snap-Off Knives

Yoshido Okada is regarded as the inventor of the snap-off knife. With his company Olfa he has developed the snap-off blade into the popular system known today and has made it popular.

In a Solingen pattern book by J. A. Henckel's Zwillingswerk from the year 1887, one can find a 41/4 and a 53/4 knife called a "break-off knife." The blade, which is fixed in the handle, has a diagonally running predetermined breaking point.

A blade with a predetermined breaking point—but now housed in a handle and slide-out—still forms the basis of all modern snap-off blade knives produced by Olfa, Stanley, or the German manufacturer Martor.

Chapter Summary

Special jobs demand special tools—this principle is also true of knives. The world of the special knife is varied and ranges from sickles and pruning knives used in agriculture to leather and grafting knives to surgical scalpels.

The safety aspect of specialty knives is of particular importance, especially in industrial use, where work is done on a piece-rate basis: to avoid accidents, knives with covered blades are preferred, or knives whose blades automatically retract into the handle after use.

Olfa of Japan made the snap-off blade knife popular. Beneath these examples is a *kiridashi* knife.

TRIVIA: THE SCALPEL: A Few Cuts

Many consider the scalpel the surgeon's most important tool, but he uses saws, forceps, and clamps much more often. The scalpel is used mainly at the beginning of the operation, for making an incision and for separating tissue. Since the finely honed blade soon loses its sharpness, scalpels are often replaced after a few cuts. Single-use blades have therefore become very popular.

Scalpels are also used for hand-cutting work requiring maximum precision in graphic design or model making. Chemists sometimes use scalpels in determining crystal structures, to cut away or remove unsightly areas.

Chapter 8.
Handle Materials:
The Right Feel

To be able to use a knife properly, it needs a sound handle. Basically any material that feels comfortable in the hand and provides the best possible grip and is durable is suitable. Sometimes optics are also important. Here is an overview of the most-important materials for knife handles.

ABS

This synthetic material (acrylnitrile-butadiene-styrene-copolymer) is thermoplastic, meaning it can be formed in a certain temperature window. It is highly impact and heat resistant and is dishwasher safe.

Aluminum

Aluminum is a light metal that is also very strong. It is therefore favored by manufacturers for making knife handles. Anodization allows the aluminum surface to be given a protective layer in a preferred color. A frequently used aluminum alloy bears the

Spanish manufacturer Pallarès Solsona equips the knives in its inexpensive Navaja series with ABS scales. On the Navaja Comun (shown), the handle is a single piece.

Many models from Swiss manufacturer Victorinox are fitted with aluminum scales: here are three models from the Alox Limited Edition 2016 in orchid violet. *Victorinox*

Italian company Extrema Ratio uses the aluminum alloy anticorodal. *Extrema Ratio*

Carbon fiber materials are characterized by low weight and high stiffness and strength: here is a model from Klötzli of Switzerland. *Klötzli*

Delrin is not only used to smooth, as on the H20 from Great Eastern Cutlery seen here. Previously it was also used to simulate deer horn. *GEC*

A high-grade folding knife from R. B. Johnson: the handle is made of mammoth ivory; the cheek, mosaic Damasteel. *R. B. Johnson*

abbreviation 6061 (corresponds to the ISO Norm A1Mg1SiCu) and is also designated aircraft aluminum.

Anticorodal

This aluminum-silicon alloy can be cast into shape. It is used by Italian knife maker Extrema Ratio to make knife handles.

Carbon Fiber

Handles made of carbon fiber are distinguished by low weight, a high degree of stiffness and strength, and a technically cool look. High-carbon materials are turned into carbon fibers in a complex process. For carbon knife handles a composite material is usually used, binding the carbon-fiber mats with epoxy resin.

Delrin

This thermoplastic material is highly abrasion and wear resistant under varying loads.

Ivory and Fossil Materials

The Convention on International Trade in Endangered Species of Wild Fauna and Flora (CITES for short, an agreement on the international trade in endangered species of wild plants and animals) is intended to regulate the trade in animals and plants (and their parts) that are threatened by extinction. Within the European Union (EU), only registered old-stock ivory with proof of origin (so-called CITES or EU certification) can be worked. This is also true for parts and products from narwhal, walrus, polar bear, and many other animals and types of wood, such as rosewood.

One should buy such products only from serious dealers. There have been cases in which protected materials have been sold with falsified certificates to well-meaning buyers.

The trade in bones and teeth of extinct species is not affected by the CITES agreements. Well-preserved mammoth skeletons, including tusks and molars, frequently appear in the permafrost of northern Siberia. As a rule these materials must be stabilized before processing, but they do produce exquisite knife handles.

A layer of vulcanized fiber between the steel and the handle is a decent way of giving a knife more class. Seen here is the TOPS Fieldcraft.

The handle of the Parang chopping knife from Fox Knives of Italy must rest particularly well in the hand. Forprene is a good choice. *Fox Knives*

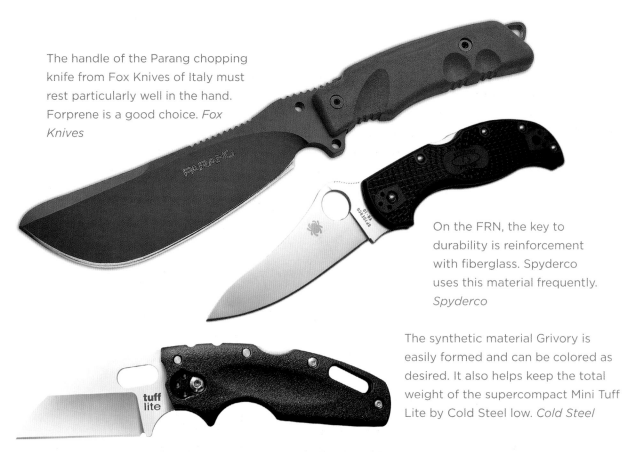

On the FRN, the key to durability is reinforcement with fiberglass. Spyderco uses this material frequently. *Spyderco*

The synthetic material Grivory is easily formed and can be colored as desired. It also helps keep the total weight of the supercompact Mini Tuff Lite by Cold Steel low. *Cold Steel*

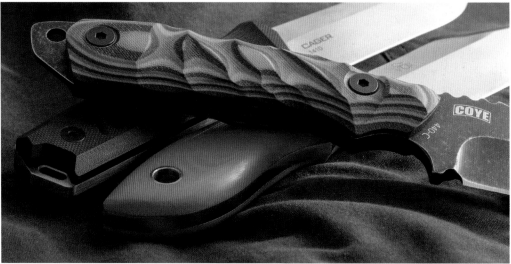

Handle scales made of G-10 are an excellent choice if low weight, strength, and grip are required.

Fiber

Typically, fiber is not used as a handle material; instead it is usually in a thin layer between the metal and the actual handle material. Vulcanized fiber has been in use since 1855, is based on paper (possibly with a cotton component), and is available in different colors. The horny material is also used for insulation, among other applications.

Forprene

This vulcanized thermoplastic elastomer has polymer content and is rubberlike.

FRN

This plastic composite material is light and durable. The English abbreviation stands for fiberglass reinforced nylon.

G-10

G-10 is a composite material created from glass fibers and synthetic resin. Because of its high stability the material is very popular, especially for knives that are exposed to high stresses and changing environmental influences.

To make G-10 glass, fiber fabrics (the individual fibers are taken from molten glass) are added to synthetic resin, shaped, and subsequently hardened. The resulting fiber-synthetic bond owes its strength and durability to the glass fibers, while its light weight is due to the epoxy resin. The outer surface of the G-10 material can be roughened or milled.

Wood is still one of the most beautiful handle materials. Stained curly birch is used on this Finnish *ahti vaara*.

Gruvory

A thermoplastic synthetic material based on PPA (polyphthalamide). It is highly temperature resistant and industry uses it as a replacement for metal in gears and gearboxes. Among its users are Cold Steel and Benchmade.

Wood

Almost every kind of wood is suitable for making knife handles: one finds on knives scales of relatively soft native woods such as pear or plum, as well as the seemingly petrified and enormously hard wood of the desert iron tree from the deserts of Arizona, or the scarcely less hard wood of the boxwood tree, which is very popular among wood turners.

Depending on the type of plant, one can use wood from branches, trunks, roots, or elsewhere. The latter is not particularly thrilling to look at. The wood of the curly birch is very popular among northern knife makers, since it becomes especially strong after special oil and heat treatment. Wood achieves long durability and resistance to environmental influences if it is stabilized (soaked in synthetic resin and allowed to harden).

Horn

Handle scales made of ram's horn, cow horn, or buffalo horn are among the classics for knife handles. The crusty outer surface structure of ram's horn provides a great look and a comfortable grip. Scales are cut mainly from the solid tips of cow or buffalo horn, after which they are polished. Deer horn is the classic material for a hunting knife; the outer layer of the horn is usually used. The horn of the South Asian sambar deer is especially dense and therefore very popular, but it has become almost impossible to obtain.

Kraton

This synthetically made polymer of styrene-ethylene/butylstyrene is very slip proof and comfortable, and safe to grip even in

Not only traditionalists swear by deer horn—the natural material also simply looks good. Sambar deer horn is used on the Linder Farmer.

When the handle must be slip proof, manufacturers such as Ontario (here the Chimera model) like to use rubberlike Kraton.

The handles of hidden-tang knives were and are often made of glued and compressed leather discs. This knife by Othello Anton Wingen Jr. dates from the 1940s.

To make Micarta, one only needs paper or linen and synthetic resin. Moki has mastered its production perfectly. The knife with the flamed bone scales also comes from this Japanese manufacturer.

Polypropylene is a synthetic material that is economical to produce. The original Svörd Peasant with L6 steel blade has a handle made of this material in bright yellow.

cold and damp. This makes it a preferred handle material for functional hunting or outdoor knives.

Bone

Bone has always been used by humans as a tool, or as a handle for tools and knives. The shin bones of cows (today usually from South America) and giraffe bone are used to make scales for knives. The bones are boiled and frequently dyed and are decorated with milled (to imitate deer horn) and flame patterns. Handles made of mammoth bone are also used on especially valuable knives.

Leather

Leather is a traditional material for making knife handles and is typically used for hidden-tang knives. Usually a sturdy holder (typically metal) is first slid over the tang and glued there. Then follow numerous pre-cut leather discs in which a hole has been cut for the tang. For visual reasons, layers of fiber or other materials can be placed be-

tween them. Glue is placed on the individual discs and they are slid into place.

The end of the handle is formed by a solid butt, which depending on the type of tang is attached with rivets or screws. Clamping devices stabilize the assembly while the glue hardens. The handle is given its final shape by using a belt sander, saw, rasp, file, or sandpaper.

Micarta

Fiber-plastic composite materials were first protected and sold at the beginning of the twentieth century under the trademark Micarta. This versatile material is characterized by low electrical conductivity and great strength, and it is used in numerous industrial areas—even as a component of spacecraft.

Micarta is made from absorbent materials bonded into a solid plate by using synthetic resin and pressure. It is particularly in demand for canvas, linen, jeans, and paper. It is warm and soft in the hand and feels very

Like Micarta, only of wood. Pakka wood is made by gluing together and pressing individual layers of wood. *Herbertz*

Paracord is a good way of improving the grip of all-steel knives, as seen on this example from Tobias Haselmayr.

By extracting the air from porous materials and then filling the spaces with thin liquid synthetic resin, one can stabilize them. This decorative piece by Laguiole en Aubrac with scales made of Koralle is one example.

POM is a good choice for cooking knives, even those that go into dishwashers. *Opinel*

Santoprene is a synthetic material with a very good grip, and it can also be given structure. Benchmade is fond of this technique. *Benchmade*

natural. This makes Micarta one of the most popular materials for knife handles.

Pakka Wood This plywood material is formed by bonding several layers of solid wood under pressure and temperature. Pakka wood is resistant to warping and shrinkage and is used mainly as a handle material on inexpensive knives.

Paracord

This tear-resistant nylon rope is used in parachute lines and consists of a braided outer layer and a continuous core, typically composed of seven thin individual strands. Fixed all-metal knives have Paracord wrapped around the grip—a functional and quick solution. Folding knives with a grommet or U-bolt are often retrofitted

with pull straps made of Paracord. There are numerous instructions and books on how to make attractive windings and lanyards.

Polypropylene

Among the most commonly used synthetic materials worldwide is thermoplastic PP, which is often used to make the handles of inexpensive knives.

POM

Polyoxymethylene is a highly molecular thermoplastic synthesized by DuPont in 1952 and patented soon afterward. It is used as a technical synthetic for precision parts on account of its stiffness and thermal stability.

CHAPTER 8. HANDLE MATERIALS: THE RIGHT FEEL

Santoprene

A soft polyurethane synthetic material that is comfortable to grip.

Stabilized Materials

Soft wood or dead wood infected with sponge on a stick, but also fossilized materials such as mammoth ivory and bones, can be very attractive in appearance. Often the basic structure of such materials is too weak, and therefore unsuitable for making knife handles unless they are stabilized: air trapped inside the material is first sucked out. The remaining pores, cracks, and fissures are subsequently filled with a thin, liquid, synthetic resin and dried (a tough elastic mixture of Plexiglas and other components is used for this purpose). Materials treated in this way become solid and moisture resistant. The synthetic resin can also easily be colored.

Titanium

Titanium combines corrosion resistance with great strength and low weight. With a strength similar to steel, it is about one-third lighter. Because of its low heat conductivity it does not feel as cold in the hand as steel or aluminum. Titanium is also hypoallergenic.

Pure titanium is generally used for scales and handles. For plates (especially on Liner Lock folding knives), the spring-hardened titanium alloy 6A14V is usually used. Some knife blades are also made of titanium, if antimagnetic and rustproof qualities are of primary importance—for example, in divers' knives used by bomb disposal services.

Zytel

Zytel is the trade name for a glass-fiber-reinforced nylon material developed by DuPont that is used in the injection molding process. Zytel is heatproof and cold-proof, shock resistant, and abrasion resistant. The outer surfaces of Zytel scales are often textured.

Chapter Summary

The material used to make a knife handle contributes to its visual appeal, and also a knife's functionality. In the past, mainly regionally available materials were used; in the northern countries of Europe these included reindeer horn and the wood of the curly birch. In southern Europe the horns of deer, rams, and ibex and, of course, woods such as olive, box, or cork oak were used. Water buffalo horn is still widespread in Southeast Asia, while deer horn is popular in Europe. For a long time, hardwoods such as guajak (pock wood tree) have been imported from South America, and in addition to boatbuilding they have been traditionally used for the handles of maritime knives.

Some particularly elegant knives have scales made of ivory or fossil materials from the bones and teeth of extinct animals. Handle windings can also produce effective handles. On modern knives one often finds handles made of durable materials such as Kraton; composite materials such as G-10, Micarta, or carbon fiber; and metals such as stainless steel, aluminum, and titanium.

Light, solid, tough, and elegant—the combination of these qualities makes titanium a popular material for high-grade knives such as the Intrepid from Chinese manufacturer Kizer.

Very toxic please: the Zytel scales on this Zombie Chopper from Ka-Bar are uniquely colored. The glass-fiber-reinforced material is almost identical to FRN.

Chapter 9.
Blade Shapes:
A Diversity of Blades

Whether a fixed knife or folding knife, without a blade nothing can be achieved. To some extent, the outline of the blade determines the knife's purpose. Knife types generally bring together a large number of blade shapes, which will be examined in more detail in the following text, since they all have their typical characteristics.

Straight-Back Blade

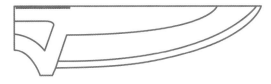

On this traditional blade form the spine runs in a straight line, while the edge follows a curve to the level of the blade spine. Familiar knife types based on this blade shape are butchers' knives, so-called *Notschlacht* and *Hippekniep* pocketknives (as previously made by many Solingen knife makers), and their American counterpart, the Sodbuster knife—the traditional pocketknife of the American farmer.

Because of its outward-curved cutting edge, the knife can be used well on flat cutting surfaces. The round-bellied area just before the point—and the relatively pronounced point—can be used very deliberately. Most *Knicker* hunting knives have a straight-back blade and are slender and elongated. Overall, the classic straight-back shape is extremely versatile.

The long rise of the cutting edge results in a bellied blade shape that one can work well with on a cutting board.

Drop Point Blade

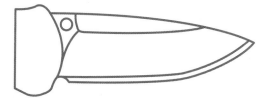

If the blade spine drops slightly in a gentle curve to the point, one is dealing with a true bestseller—the drop point blade is one of the most commonly used of all blade shapes.

This is because it is extremely versatile. In the area of the point, the edge still has sufficient "belly" to use the blade effectively in a pulling and swaying motion on a cutting board. While the point is not particularly accentuated, it can be used for thrusting and boring. Hunters gladly use drop point blades, since with them they can open the belly area of their prey without damaging internal organs. Hunters use the knife with the edge facing up and grip the blade so short that the index finger rests on the spine just before, or even over the point. This provides a high degree of control while cutting and shields the point.

The *Berger*, *Bourbonnais*, and *feuille de sauge* (sage leaf shaped, more pointed than the *Bourbonnais*)—traditional drop point variants—are found on traditional folding knives from France. The blade point can be somewhat higher than the blade's longitudinal axis or somewhat lower.

A short, slender blade in drop point shape is called a pen blade and is also useful for sharpening pencils.

On a modified drop point blade, the basic shape is slightly changed: for example, the dropping spine is thinned into a false edge—a prominent but not sharp bevel.

Spearpoint (Center Point) Blade

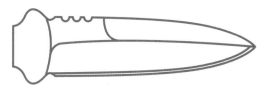

The spearpoint blade is a variant of the drop point blade. The spine drops away toward the point while the cutting edge rises, and the two meet in the center of the blade height. This typically results in a slender pointed blade. Because of its central position, the point can be used in a well-controlled fashion.

Dagger Blade

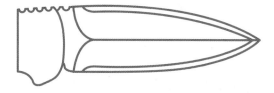

A dagger-shaped blade is found mainly on stabbing weapons. It has a central point and is ground on both sides: both the descending spine and rising main edge are sharpened. This results in a symmetrical blade shape that is particularly slender and comes to a

The M16-03, with its spearpoint blade, is a classic from the CRKT catalog. *CRKT*

The Böker Speedlock (here the Army model) uses a textbook drop point blade. *Böker*

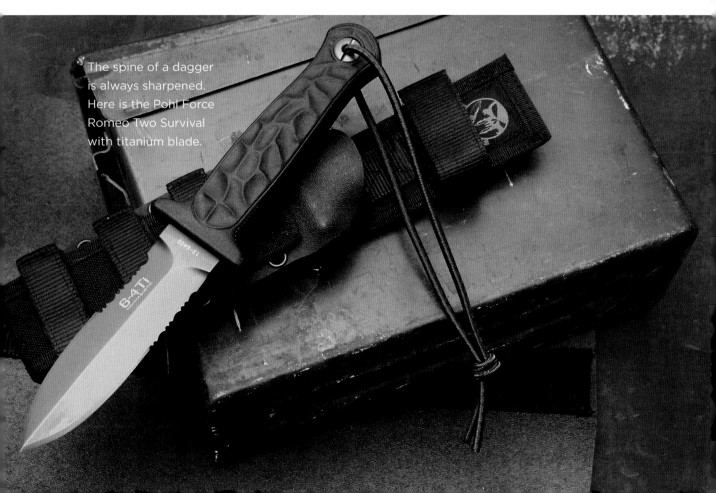

The spine of a dagger is always sharpened. Here is the Pohl Force Romeo Two Survival with titanium blade.

The pike blade has a pronounced point with a bellied cutting edge. The Klaas Monolith implements this elegant shape masterfully. *Stefan Schmalhaus*

The sheep's-foot blade, with its straight cutting edge and arc-shaped descending spine, is a popular blade shape for maritime use. The knives shown here come from Tina, Strider, and Lütters.

point, making penetration easy. Its practical uses are very limited, since the sharpened blade spine harbors considerable potential for self-injury and the point is sometimes so fragile that it cannot be used for robust work.

Clip Point (Bowie) Blade

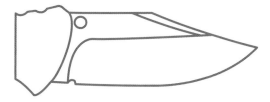

Clip point blades have the appearance of having the forward third of the blade "clipped" off. The clip itself can be straight or concave. The point is usually slightly above the blade's longitudinal axis. Because this type of blade was typical for the legendary bowie knife, it is sometimes also called the bowie blade (whether Jim Bowie's original bowie knife actually had this blade shape is not certain).

The pronounced point can be used very nimbly and precisely. Whether one wishes to stick or pick something up or remove a splinter, the fine clip point blade can handle it. At the same time, thanks to the bellied cutting edge, the blade can also be used effectively on a cutting surface. Of course the finer the point, the more sensitive it is.

Special forms of the clip point blade are the long and slender *yatagan* (the name comes from an Ottoman saber) typically used for the French Laguiole knife and the pronounced "Turkish" blade found on the French *douk douk*.

Sheep's-Foot Blade

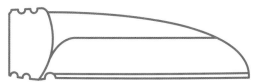

Watespitz—the Solingen name for this blade—says it all: on this blade form the point is at the level of the straight *wate* (bevel), the cutting edge. The rounded spine drops sharply, making this type of blade quite unsuitable for stabbing. In part for this reason, this type of blade is favored for maritime knives—no one wants to come amiss with his own blade point in heavy seas. Although the point cannot be used for stabbing, it can be used effectively for a variety of tasks, such as cutting tarpaulins, sail cloths, or foils.

The straight cutting edge brings with it advantages and disadvantages: the sheep's-foot blade falls behind when working on a flat cutting surface, because practically only the point can be used. On the other hand, for carving or freehand cutting the straight edge allows a great deal of force to be transferred during straight cuts.

In English-speaking areas, a slender sheep's-foot blade with an angled point is called a coping blade. It is frequently found on electricians' knives, where it is used for making cuts in the covers of cables or to open packages.

If the point of a skinner blade is dropped, like on this Meyerco, it is called a semiskinner. *Meyerco*

Wharncliffe Blade

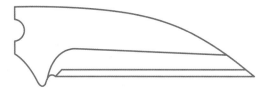

The designation of Wharncliffe for a blade form first appeared among knife makers in Sheffield in the first half of the nineteenth century. There was also at that time a Lord Wharncliffe who may have given it its name. Its elegant shape is definite: the edge is completely straight, while the blade spine—relatively tapering—falls away to the point. The pronounced point is the main difference from the sheep's-foot blade, with which it otherwise shares basic characteristics. Wharncliffe blades make an elegant impression and are very versatile.

Trailing-Point Blade

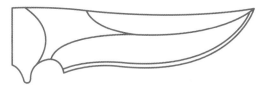

This blade type is used almost exclusively on skinning knives used by hunters. Because the point is clearly above the line of the blade spine, the rising cutting edge has a great deal of belly and can be used effectively to remove skin with pulling cuts.

Tanto Blade

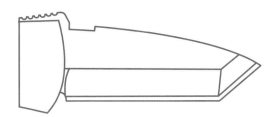

A *tanto* was originally a fighting knife with blades up to 1 foot long used by Japanese

These two models from Fantoni of Italy display a very elegant combined form of drop point and Wharncliffe blades.

From traditional Japanese armor piercer to style maker; the *tanto* blade has a long history behind it. These two CRKT models (M16 and K.I.S.S.) demonstrate the angular American form.

In contrast to other blades with a straight cutting edge, *kiridashi* blades can also be used effectively on flat cutting surfaces. This custom knife was made by Stefan Richle.

A hook-shaped blade is often found on agricultural implements, where they are used in pulling cuts. Here is an old Lütters grafting knife.

samurai. The original typically had a straight spine and a round, rising cutting edge. So-called armor stabbers, *tantos* were particularly sturdy.

In the mid-1980s, the adapted American tanto shape became popular on the knife scene, and since then it has been a permanent element of catalogs of all major manufacturers. The blade of the American tanto retains full blade thickness until just before the point. The majority of the cutting edge runs straight, then rises at an angle to the point—also in a straight line. This is the difference from the Japanese original. The point can be at spine height or below it. The blade cross section is usually especially sturdy, and the point is also consciously made robust.

Kiridashi Blade

Kiridashi blades are found mainly on Japanese woodworking knives. A characteristic is its angular shape, the result of the cutting edge rising in a straight line to the point at roughly 45 to 60 degrees. This accentuated point allows the user to undertake precise scribing and carving work. The straight edge enables exact carving and controlled cuts to be carried out. The relatively large angle between the longitudinal axis of the handle and the cutting edge provides improved knuckle clearance when one is working on a flat surface.

Hawkbill Blade

The hawkbill blade form is quite unsuitable for cutting activities on a cutting board or work surface. For carving, or for cutting and scribing, the hawkbill blade is in its element. The point is "ripping" and can usually be forced under tight bindings. The claw-shaped point—depending on the degree of curve—prevents the binding from slipping away and allows a great deal of force to be transferred to the inner radius. Because of this inner radius, the usable cutting-edge length is clearly longer than the linear connection between the point and the beginning of the blade.

Curved, pointed blades are typical of sickles, gardening and pruning knives, and *karambit* knives as used in many knife-fighting techniques, and for certain work, such as hunting and rescue knives. They are especially well suited to cutting ropes and belts.

The award-winning Profi Rescue Tool from Hubertus relies on an especially safe blade form and an automatic opening mechanism.

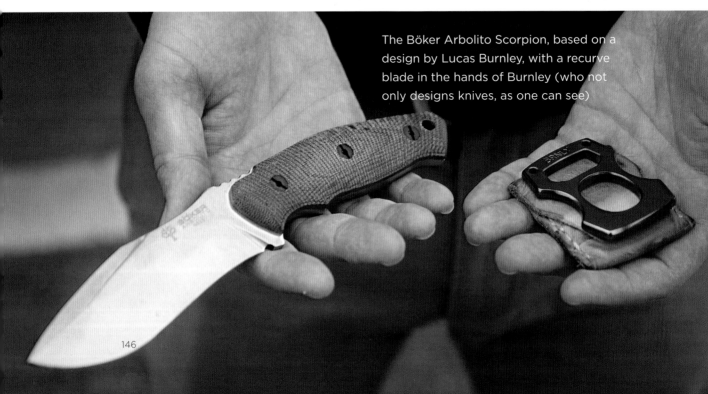

The Böker Arbolito Scorpion, based on a design by Lucas Burnley, with a recurve blade in the hands of Burnley (who not only designs knives, as one can see)

146

Rescue Blade

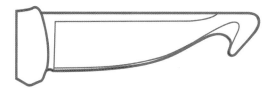

In emergency situations there is usually excitement, and quick action is required. To minimize the risk to oneself and to the person involved in the accident, many rescue blades have no point. Where the point usually is, there is instead a rounded curve to avoid stabbing injuries or unintentional piercing of sensitive materials. Typically the blade is shaped like a hook in this area, with its inner radius ground. This allows it to be safely used to cut belts or items of clothing. Sometimes the rest of the edge is also ground sharp.

Recurve Blade

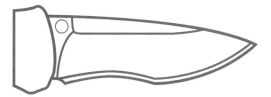

If the cutting edge of a knife has two curvatures—like an *S* on its side—then one is describing a recurve blade. If the curvatures are especially pronounced, then the cutting length is clearly greater than the linear distance between the point and the beginning of the blade. The S shape also produces different effective areas along the edge, such as an especially high transfer of force on the material to be cut at the junction of an inner curvature to an outer one.

Chapter Summary

Across all types of knives there are numerous basic blade shapes named for their external outline. To a large extent it determines what the knife is well or less well suited for. Among the most-popular blade shapes are the drop point and the clip point forms.

On the sturdy drop point blade, the blade spine falls away to the point with an outer curvature, while the bellied cutting edge rises. Drop point blades are very versatile and thus very popular—even among hunters.

On a clip point blade, the blade spine descends in a straight or concave line. Here too the cutting edge rises bellied to the point. The result is a more flexible and clearly more pointed basic shape that makes an elegant impression. Legendary folding knives such as the Buck Hunter 110 and most bowie knives have clip point blades.

Blades with straight cutting edges, such as sheep's-foot or Wharncliffe blades, are especially easy to sharpen and permit a controlled transfer of force along their entire blade length. This blade shape is less suitable for cutting on a flat surface because one can only scratch with the point instead of cutting properly.

Chapter 10. Factors in Cutting Ability: The Science of Cutting

It is primarily the shape and preparation of the cutting edge and the remaining blade cross section that determine how well one can cut, carve, or chop. Learn here what physically takes place during cutting and what relationships there are between the ability to cut and the robustness of a blade.

The Cutting Edge

Before the basic blade cross section comes into play, the part of the blade that first contacts the material to be cut does its job. On a knife that is the cutting edge. The thinner this is, the sharper the blade. The cutting edge concentrates the force of the hand wielding the knife on the material to be cut. If the pressure exerted is great enough to separate the molecular structure of the material being cut—the rope, the piece of wood, apple, or whatever—then one cuts. That is what it comes down to.

The cutting edge itself always has a certain width prescribed by the structure of the steel and the fineness of the abrasive material. Thicknesses of a few thousandths of a millimeter (high-grade razor blades are

just 0.0005 mm) are possible. This alone reveals how impressive a raw-material steel is. For a blade that must cut harder materials, the cutting edge must be thicker. Otherwise it would be too easily damaged.

From the actual cutting edge, the flanks separate in a V shape. This area is called the cutting bevel. The cutting bevel is important for providing "rear cover" for the cutting edge. The angle between the flanks (the cutting angle) determines the strength of the cutting edge. At the same time it determines the ease with which the blade cuts.

The parameters of strength and cutting performance are unfortunately opposed. A coarse cutting angle results in a stronger edge than a finer cutting angle. On the other hand, with a fine cutting angle one can cut better than with a coarse one. It is therefore important to find a suitable balance independent of the expected load and the blade steel.

The edge of a knife blade of fine-grain steel—with which one can cut softer materials—can have a cutting angle of about

The Geometry of the Knife Blade

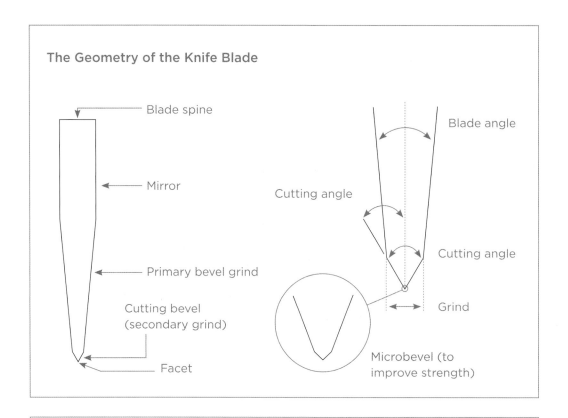

Blade spine

Mirror

Primary bevel grind

Cutting bevel
(secondary grind)

Facet

Blade angle

Cutting angle

Cutting angle

Grind

Microbevel (to
improve strength)

The Geometry of the Knife Blade

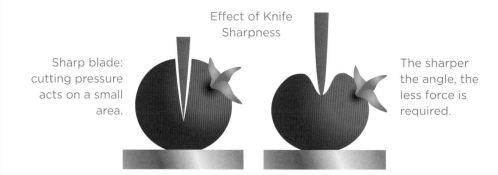

Effect of Knife
Sharpness

Sharp blade:
cutting pressure
acts on a small
area.

The sharper
the angle, the
less force is
required.

Obtuse blade: cutting pressure is dispersed over a greater area.
A question of thickness: the narrower the cutting edge, the less force is required to
separate the molecular bonds of the material being cut.

20 degrees. This means that each flank has an angle of 10 degrees to the vertical axis. For a knife blade that must stand up to greater stresses, 30 to 50 degrees (total angle) is a practical figure.

Smooth or Serrated Edge?

When it comes to cutting performance, in addition to the cutting angle, the edge grind is also important: it can be done as a smooth, plain edge or as a serrated edge. A smooth edge exhibits no irregularities—normally the cutting edge is made so straight and smooth that even under powerful microscopes it is as uniform as possible. The smooth cutting edge is the traditional form and still the standard grind.

Knives with serrated edges have been an integral part of the catalogs of major knife manufacturers for decades. In addition to a smooth version, most of their bestsellers are offered with a partly or fully serrated edge. Serrated edges are good form on rescue knives and tactical knives. The former are almost exclusively made with sharper serrations.

There are different forms of serrated blades, but one thing is almost always identical: the blade consists of a series of serrations joined by concave ground surfaces. If one places such a blade on a flat surface, only the serrations touch. These are usually sturdily formed and work with a "ripping" cut.

In detail there are differences. Some manufacturers grind the recesses in a constant format. Others alternate between smaller and larger inner radii. And the serrations between them can also be alternately rounded and sharp edged.

Among the advantages of a serrated blade is that the peaks and valleys lengthen the effective blade, compared to a similarly shaped blade with a linear cutting edge.

Even hard cutting surfaces scarcely dull a serrated blade, since it always rests solely on the serrations, protecting the sharpness of the inner radii. This is why steak knives in restaurants are often serrated. A serrated

A smooth edge produces a finer cut than a serrated one. *left: Fox, right: Spyderco*

blade—like a saw—cuts by the back-and-forth motion of the blade. Great pressure is not necessary. The material is "gripped" relatively easily by the serrations and is subsequently cut by the concave cutting edges.

If hard synthetic materials or thin metal must be cut, standard blades with a smooth edge frequently slide over the surface or quickly become dull. No so with the serrated blade, which even when dull remains relatively usable, since the sturdy serrations continue to "rip."

One might ask oneself why smooth edges are even needed. The answer is quite simple: a well-sharpened smooth blade is superior, or at least equal to, a serrated blade in almost all areas. A sharp, smooth blade produces a finer cross section and does not become caught as easily. And the sharpening of smooth blades is less complicated than sharpening serrated blades. To do so exactly as prescribed, one must sharpen every hollow individually, requiring a round or half-round whetstone profile with a matching diameter.

In short, wood carvers and cutting aesthetes depend on smooth cutting. Anyone who often finds oneself confronted by fibrous or synthetic materials and has no time to sharpen—or if in an emergency all that matters is cutting through materials—is well served by a serrated blade. Not all serrated blades are the same. The tempered versions, such as those offered by Victorinox, Spyderco, and CRKT, work well in practice.

The Most-Important Knife Grinds

How well one can cut, or cut through, and how sturdy the blade is overall depends in large part on the basic grind of the blade—its cross-section profile. With a blade that is very thin from the spine to the edge, one can cut many materials more easily than with an equally sharp but clearly thicker blade: one cuts more easily through the material, while the other rubs and wedges itself and therefore requires more force.

One thing is clear, however: a blade with a 6-millimeter-thick (0.02 inch) spine has more strength reserves. In an emergency it can even be used as a pry bar. One is better off not to try this with a 2-millimeter-thick (0.007 inch) blade. The balance between cutting ability and strength is just a compromise. Actually this is true of every part of a knife, from the choice of a suitable steel to the shape of the handle.

If the blade flanks come together from the spine, or from a lower-placed bevel edge in a V shape, it is called a flat grind. On closer examination, one distinguishes between the primary bevel (the hollow grind) and the secondary bevel (on the edge), which has a rather obtuse angle.

If the primary bevel extends to the cutting edge without further changes of angle (with no secondary bevel), then it is referred to as a zero grind. Scandinavian knives are traditionally shaped this way. This grind produces a very small cutting angle and a correspondingly high degree of sharpness.

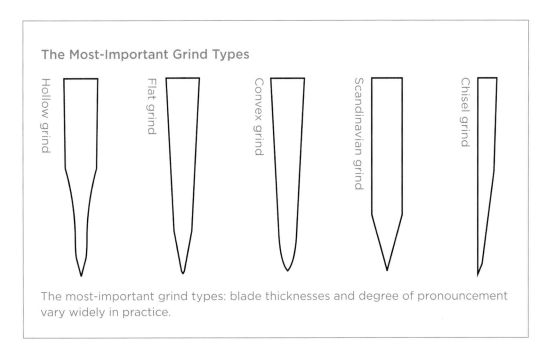

The Most-Important Grind Types

Hollow grind

Flat grind

Convex grind

Scandinavian grind

Chisel grind

The most-important grind types: blade thicknesses and degree of pronouncement vary widely in practice.

Blade angle and blade thickness play an important role in deeper cuts.

On a hollow-grind blade, the blade sides are concave. This is achieved by using a round stone for grinding. The smaller its radius, the more pronounced the hollow grind. The greater the grinding-stone radius, the more moderate the hollow grind.

The cutting bevel (secondary bevel) is ground flat in a V shape. "Zero ground" hollow grinds with no secondary bevel are almost nonexistent because of their sensitivity.

The convex grind is characterized by the convex flanks of the blade. The flanks come together in arch form and form the cutting edge where they meet. There are very convex grinds (e.g., on splitting axes) and moderately convex grinds, such as one occasionally finds on outdoor knives. The latter are mostly of the high-grade sort, since a convex blade requires manual labor.

Each of these grind types has its justifications: a well-made hollow-ground blade thickens slowly from the cutting edge and therefore penetrates very well initially. This is also advantageous for sharpening. At some point, provided it is relatively strong, the blade abruptly becomes much thicker and then it possibly wedges, regardless of the qualities of the material being cut.

The convex grind is usually designed for splitting and displacing. Its greatest advantage is the blade's strength (for the same grind height), resulting in a relatively powerful profile.

The flat grind is the midpoint between hollow grind and convex grind and offers a good compromise of strength and cutting ability. It is therefore very popular. It can be finely pronounced for high cutting performance or more obtuse for higher loads.

On many knives, one finds a cutting bevel that is ground slightly convex, even though the blade cross section has a flat or hollow grind. This is simply due to the medium with which the cutting edge was ground. Sharpening by hand with a whetstone automatically produces a convex blade, because one can never maintain the same angle consistently. This effect is quite desirable, because it increases the strength of the cutting edge and makes it less likely to break when it contacts hard cutting materials.

Influence of Coatings on the Blade Surface

In addition to its shape, the surface characteristics of a blade are important to its cutting characteristics. Polished or at least finely smoothed blades produce less friction. Coatings such as Teflon have the same effect. But blade flanks intentionally left bare can also bring advantages: the adherence of soft foodstuffs to cooking knives can be reduced, improving the "food release factor."

The sides of a blade with a convex grind bulge outward slightly. Also, many knives have convex-grind cutting edges (knives by Tobias Haselmayr, Tina, and Svörd).

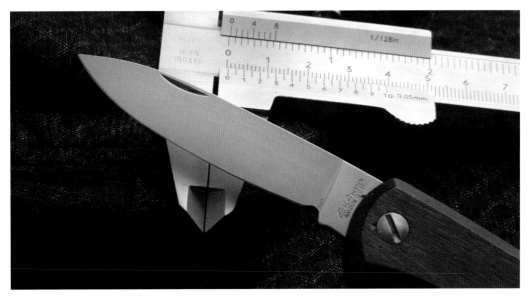

The grind—the blade thickness above the cutting edge—has a great influence on cutting ability.

Chapter Summary

How well one can cut something is initially determined by the lower part of the blade: the cutting edge. The thickness of the cutting edge and the angle of the subsequent cutting bevel have a direct influence on the amount of force that one must apply to separate the molecular compounds of the material being cut.

How well one can cut deep into the material is determined mainly by the cross section of the blade. On knives, one finds the V-shaped flat grind, the concave hollow grind, and the outwardly curved convex grind. All grind types have their advantages and disadvantages.

Whether the blade is ground smooth or serrated also has an influence on how well one cuts. The surface characteristics of the blade also play a role. Manufacturers therefore use friction-reducing coatings or add holes in the blade, especially on cheese knives.

Coatings with good antifriction properties are used to reduce friction between the blade and the material being cut. Böker uses Ilafon on these Speedlock models.

A fine cutting angle typical of Scandinavian knives is advantageous for cutting.

Chapter 11.
Knife Steel: A Very Special Material

In few other aspects of the world of knives are there so many—in part contradictory—opinions as the choice of the proper knife steel. There are books devoted entirely to this subject. And yes, one cannot gain a knowledge of knife steel at a single glance. But don't worry: a degree in physics or chemistry is not required for a basic understanding. A little knowledge is sufficient to provide you with the tools to become a knife expert. In this chapter you will learn how steel is made, how it is made into knives, and for which knives it is suitable.

From Iron Ore to Sheet Steel

Our modern world would simply not be conceivable without steel. Steel is the basis of almost all machines and tools, construction steel supports our tallest buildings, and sheet steel is used to make cars and ships.

There is also no getting around steel in the making of knife blades. For making durable blades capable of keeping an edge, there is no other material with so many desirable qualities. Good steel can be milled to a few thousandths of a millimeter and, in the process, becomes so hard—and at the same time tough—that one can cut not only fruit, vegetables, and meat with it, but also hardwoods, plastics, and fibrous materials such as cardboard or sisal rope.

Many steps are required before iron ore—most of which now comes from Brazil or China—becomes a knife blade. The iron ore is delivered to steel mills by rail and sea. There the ore is initially turned into pig iron in a blast furnace and then through the addition of alloying elements is turned into molten steel at temperatures in excess of 2,000°C (3,632°F).

Steel for knife-making hobbyists is usually sold as flat steel in annealed form, making it easier to work. At the very end it gains its hardness through tempering.

Swedish steel producer Sandvik first turns iron ore into pig iron and then in huge furnaces makes it into molten steel with the addition of scrap steel.

The special composition of iron and other alloying elements, such as carbon and chromium, produce certain alloys that are formed into round material, plates, or steel bands.

But steel is not just steel. To be able to meet the most different requirements, there are hundreds of steel varieties. Engineers control the exact quantities of iron and other alloying elements (the most important are carbon, chromium, molybdenum, and vanadium) that are to be part of the steel. This fine tuning is in large part responsible for the later qualities of the finished steel.

The smelting process in the steel mill results in blocks of steel weighing tons. These slabs are again heated until red hot and then rolled into sheets of different thicknesses or reshaped into round material. Anyone who has the opportunity to visit a steel mill should do so. The sheer size of the buildings, the noise, the heat—all of this is truly impressive.

From Sheet Steel to Blade

Sheet steel containing necessary alloying elements forms the starting point for the majority of knives made industrially or manually. Large knife manufacturers buy steel by the ton, while knife makers can purchase it in handy sizes through distributors. An 8-inch-long piece of 12C27 Swedish steel 1.25 inches wide and 0.15 inches thick can be had for less than twelve dollars (10 Euros).

To make the steel easier to work, and to save wear on tools, it is delivered untempered. Individual knife makers then saw or file the steel into the basic shape of the knife and work the knife on a belt grinder or file. Material is removed until the tang achieves its desired shape and the blade receives its basic grind. Well-equipped

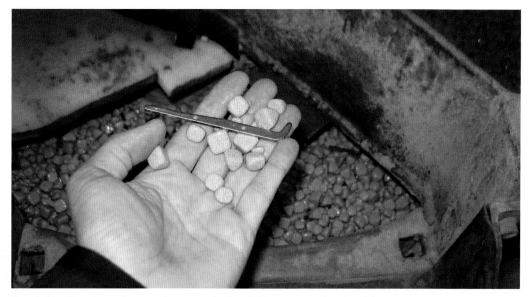

Tumbling involves the steel parts of a knife being "washed" with abrasive ceramic bodies for hours. This smooths traces left by stamping and other work.

Forging is the oldest form of knife making. The smith heats the steel to forming temperature in a coal fire and subsequently works it with a hammer.

The anvil is one of the smith's most important tools. On it the steel is formed into a knife with aimed blows.

professional knife makers also use special grinding machines or computer-controlled milling machines for this task.

Smiths heat the steel in a forge until it is red hot and can be shaped with hammer blows on an anvil. The objective during forging is to come as close as possible to the ultimate shape of the knife. The final shape is also achieved using a belt grinder, file, or emery cloth.

The manual production of knives requires elbow grease, sheets of sandpaper, and much time. The expenditure should not be underestimated, and it explains the high price. Anyone who ever makes a knife will in the future see knives through different eyes.

Depending on what the handle is later supposed to look like, smiths and knife makers use a drill press to drill holes in the tang or cut threads for the later installation of handle scales or a handle. Then the knife is tempered, cleaned, and smoothed again and finally is sharpened.

Industrially these processes are carried out mechanically. To make flat-tang knives, the later knife shape is stamped from sheet steel or cut out by laser or water jet. Then robotic grinders or specialists take over the forming of the knife, the basic grind, and all other work, such as surface processing and attaching the handle.

In the forge, the steel is shaped as far as possible into a knife with a hammer. The knife's shape can also be created by removing material with files or a belt grinder.

TRIVIA: TEMPERING: Decisive Factor

Blade steel must be tempered so that it can be used for cutting long term. This process involves several stages of tempering. First the steel is heated. At a steel-specific temperature between 800°C and 1,200°C (1,470ºF–2,190ºF), the microscopic structure of the steel is put in a state of turmoil. The carbon, which in soft steel is bonded to iron, disperses and spreads itself within the microscopic structure of the steel. The resulting uniform structure is called austenite.

If the steel is cooled abruptly (in water or oil, though cool air suffices for some types of steel), the free carbon atoms are virtually "overpowered"; they do not find their way back to their original position and are trapped in new microscopic structures (called martensite). It is precisely this that makes steel hard. Sometimes it becomes so hard that one can scribe glass with it. It would shatter if it fell on the ground. A subsequent controlled addition of heat releases the surfeit of tensions and results in a steel that is still hard, but more durable.

So-called selective tempering is a special case: the result is a blade that is hard in the area of the cutting edge, but whose spine is soft and elastic. Japanese *tanto* and *katana* are traditionally tempered this way. The process creates a *hamon*, a visible temper line that separates the highly tempered part of the blade from the softer part.

The areas of the blade that should remain soft (spine and parts of the flanks) are covered with an insulating layer of clay before tempering. They thus cool more slowly than the cutting edge during quenching. The advantage: before a selectively tempered blade breaks, a deformation takes place that is sometimes reversible. A thoroughly tempered blade will break when its load limit is exceeded.

A blade covered in this way cools selectively. Only the cutting edge is cooled so abruptly that it becomes hard.

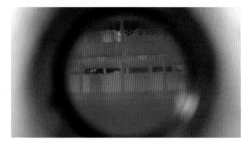

At commercial heat-treating companies, blades and other steel components are brought to necessary temperature in a hardening oven.

The blade and handle are subsequently ground again and finely smoothed. Then all that remains is to grind the edge. Some manufacturers check the requirements with respect to cutting angle and the precision of the grind with the help of laser technology. Usually all that remains is to etch the company logo and information about the steel on the blade, and then the knives are packaged and dispatched for sale.

Types of Steel and Technical Terms

The shape and cross section of a blade determine to a large degree how well one can cut with it. The blade geometry is the spirit of the knife. But no matter how willing the spirit, if the body (in this case the steel) is too weak, the whole is nothing.

The composition of a steel type is an indication of its potential. The steel's composition of iron (Fe), carbon (C), and other alloying elements determines its most-important qualities: hardness, wear resistance, resilience, maximum sharpness and fineness, rust resistance, and sharpenability. By far the most important element is carbon. It is this element that turns iron into steel and ensures that it can be turned into a workpiece. Approximately 0.3 percent carbon is necessary in the steel microstructure. The upper limit is about 2 percent.

Classification of Steels

Most knife users do not have an extensive knowledge of steel. "Steel is steel" goes the saying. Ask someone on the street which steel it is, and one will perhaps hear "Solingen steel," which is nonsense, because steel was never produced in Solingen. Perhaps some know that there are stainless and non-stainless steels. Or Damascus—allegedly the best steel of all, from which expensive and almost invincible samurai blades were made. Even in discussions among knowledgeable knife fans, facts are often twisted. The subject is in fact that complex.

The steel mills produce defined types of steel with a specific composition. In Germany they are given a material number (such as 1.4116) and a DIN designation (such as X50CrMoV15, indicating the same type of steel). There is also the American AISI standard, according to which the steel types 440C and 154-CM are designated, as well as Japanese steel types such as AUS-8 or ATS-34 to the current JIS standard. All systems and designations coexist and are used interchangeably.

To top it all, manufacturers also market their knives with trade names such as Elmax (a powder-metallurgical steel from Sweden) or M390 (another powder-metallurgical steel from Austrian manufacturer Böhler). When some manufacturers use fantasy names for their blade steels (such as XT 80) or good-sounding but insignificant names such as surgeon's steel, then the chaos is perfect.

Another frequently used term is stainless steel. In the vernacular this is understood to mean a really rustproof steel (usually a chrome-nickel such as 18-10; i.e., for kitchen

TRIVIA: CERAMIC BLADES: Harder Than Steel

As one of humanity's oldest cultural techniques, the making of ceramics is rooted deep in our history: 10,000-year-old plastics made of burnt clay and true works of art made of porcelain prove this. The manufacturer of precise ceramic blades has nothing to do with this.

Modern technical ceramics used for efficient blades consist of synthetically made metal oxide of the highest purity and quality. Zirconium oxide ceramic is a hard material that cannot be ground with customary materials such as silicon carbide. Only diamond has sufficient hardness to be able to grind ceramic blades. To form the ceramic material, the oxide ceramic particles are "baked together" under high pressure at temperatures far in excess of 1,000°C (1,832°F). The shaping and grinding of the blade are then accomplished with diamond abrasives.

Blades made of zirconium oxide are enormously hard—harder than any steel. They are just below that of diamonds. Ceramic blades are also light, extremely wear resistant, and absolutely corrosion proof. When used properly, they can retain their sharpness for years of use. The smoothness of the ceramic material also results in less friction when cutting. Since the material neither gives nor absorbs odors, it is sufficient to rinse the knife in water. It is therefore a popular material for kitchen knives.

Working with a good ceramic knife is a pleasure. Such knives are clearly susceptible to breakage. An accidental contact with stony ground and perhaps the tip is gone. It also cannot be used as a lever under any circumstances.

High-grade ceramic knives (here from world market leader Kyocera) can clearly withstand more stress than one would think.

This abrading manila rope was cut 1,000 times without causing any serious loss of sharpness to the ceramic blade.

underside of a porcelain plate, was surely made of such a simple steel.

Alloying, together with heat treatment, also influences whether there are carbides in the steel microstructure and what it looks like. Carbides are microscopically small particles with diameters of between 1/1000 and 1/20 of a millimeter. They are created by combining carbon with other elements such as iron, chrome, or tungsten. They are clearly harder than the steel microstructure in which they are embedded.

Carbides form during the tempering process, and also during the smelting process. Even minor additions of chrome, vanadium, or tungsten lead to the formation of carbides. The number, hardness, size, and distribution of carbides in the steel microstructure help determine how wear resistant a steel is and how thin and fine it can be ground. To be anchored stably, the carbides must be surrounded by sufficient steel. Otherwise they will too easily chip from a knife edge. Steel varieties with a high density of large carbides can therefore not be ground as finely as steels with small or even no carbides.

For steel gourmets who insist on the finest cuts, only steels without carbides, or with a very equal distribution of small carbides, can really be considered. These are the unalloyed or low-alloy steels that are not rustproof. There are also several highly alloyed rustproof steels that are relatively fine grained.

The Most-Important Steel Properties
Hardness

The hardness of a blade is measured and stated as an HRC value (Hardness Rockwell C). The measurement is made by pressing a specially formed diamond cone into the steel at a specified pressure. The less the depth of penetration of the diamond cone, the harder the steel.

How hard a blade can become is largely dependent on the carbon content of the steel. Values between 52 and 65 HRC are found in knife blades. Whether a blade should be soft or hard depends on its purpose: a relatively soft blade will give under heavy loads and bend permanently, but it does not break. A highly tempered steel can withstand a high loading and bends very elastically, but at some point it breaks. Shock-like loads and lateral bending in particular lead to breakages in the cutting edge of highly tempered blades. A high degree of hardness does have a positive

To determine the hardness of a blade, a diamond cone is pressed into steel at a prescribed pressure, and the depth of penetration is subsequently measured.

TRIVIA: COATINGS: Protection against Rust and More

In the making of machines and tools, they (including their edges) are often coated with materials much harder than steel that have a particularly smooth and therefore low-friction surface structure. The harder the coating, the longer it can counteract wear, and the less the friction, the less the resulting heat.

The coating of knife blades is done mainly to protect against rust. Coatings on military blades are also designed to prevent unwanted reflections. Low-friction characteristics are primarily a factor in designing kitchen knives.

The following coatings are most commonly used:

▶ fluoropolymer coatings: Among the outstanding qualities of this coating process (PTFE, FEP, PFA) are outstanding antistick characteristics and a very low gliding-friction coefficient. Teflon is a product designation by Dupont and the best-known product in this category. The Teflon coating is also foodstuff approved (FDA, EG 1935/2004).

▶ powder coatings: Powder coatings are based primarily on epoxy or polyester resins. The powder is electrostatically charged—opposite to the blade steel—and applied with a spray gun. The powder settles onto the steel, sticks there electrostatically, and forms the powder coating. The hardening and stable attachment are achieved by subsequent baking at temperatures of up to 200°C (390ºF).

▶ DLC (diamond-like carbon) coating: This diamond-like carbon coating is applied by the chemical vapor deposition (CVD) or physical vapor deposition (PVD) method, usually in a vacuum. It forms a highly interconnected carbon matrix and combines a high level of hardness with great elasticity. Hardnesses of up to 6000 HV (Vickers hardness) are achieved.

▶ titanium coatings: Coatings such as titanium carbonitride (TiCN) and titanium nitride (TiN) are applied using the PVD (physical vapor deposition) method. The coating material is heated in a vacuum to a gaseous state. It then condenses on the surface of the steel.

▶ tungsten carbide coatings: Hard metal coatings with tungsten carbide are applied by thermal spraying, using flame-spraying or high-speed flame-spraying techniques. In both coating methods the tungsten carbide is sprayed onto the steel and grips the previously irradiated material.

▶ ceramic coatings: Ceramic-based coatings are very convincing in their corrosion protection, ability to resist wear, hardness, and durability. A well-known US brand is Cerakote, which is applied to a previously treated metal surface, after which it must be dried and cured in an oven or kiln.

A selectively hardened blade by Tobias Haselmayr after the hardest stress test: the heavy hammer blows have bent the chucked blade, but it did not completely break in two.

Nonrustproof carbon steel is very popular among fans of resilient blades that can be ground to a fine edge. It requires some care; otherwise it will look like this after a night in its leather sheath.

effect on the cutting edge's life, or how long a blade retains its usable sharpness. Other terms for this are edge retention and cutting-edge stability.

Wear Resistance

Wear resistance is an indicator of how well a cutting edge can withstand the mechanical wear caused by hard and abrasive particles embedded in the material being cut. The level of wear resistance depends on the hardness, and in particular the composition of the steel. Carbides embedded in the steel are the decisive factor.

If one must cut materials with hard inclusions, such as cardboard, sisal rope, or a skin embedded with sand and small stones, then a high degree of wear resistance has great advantages. The more wear resistant a steel is, the longer it takes to sharpen and the higher demands the sharpening tool must be able to withstand.

Resiliency

Resiliency is understood as the quality of steel not to break or crack under high impact or bending stresses, and to offer a certain resistance to these stresses. A steel's molecular construction is of primary importance: the more fine grained the steel, the better its resiliency. The more coarse grained a steel is and the nearer it is to its individual maximum hardness, the more brittle it is.

Corrosion Resistance

Acids and water in combination with oxygen are the natural enemies of steel blades, since they result in oxidation processes. The result is rust. If this decomposition affects the cutting edge (which is often only a few thousandths of a millimeter wide), it can lead to weakening, and consequently a more rapid dulling.

Corrosion-resistant steels clearly resist oxidation better than non-corrosion-proof steels. Chrome not bound in carbide form with a content of at least 10.5 percent creates the condition for a very high corrosion resistance.

Another advantage of a corrosion-resistant steel is its taste neutrality and its visual appearance: non-corrosion-proof steel can—especially when cutting acidic foods—give a metallic taste and tarnish blue gray.

Nevertheless, many users cannot be talked out of their non-corrosion-proof knives. This is mainly because, with proper care, one can avoid the occurrence of rust, and because non-corrosion-proof steel usually has very good mechanical qualities. Also, coatings are relatively effective in preventing rust. With such knives one needs to care only for the cutting edge, since this is not coated.

Fineness of the Microstructure

The more fine grained a steel is, the more pointed and thinner one can grind the blade. This is of vital importance for the sharpness of a blade. At the same time, fine-grained steels are easier to sharpen than those with a coarser composition.

Fineness of grain is—assuming correct tempering—determined by the steel's

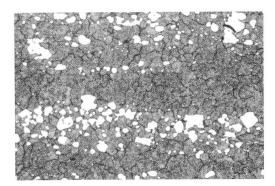

Carbides (*white*) are harder than the microstructure of steel and are created by combining carbon with other elements such as iron, chromium, or vanadium. Seen here is a carbide-rich steel.

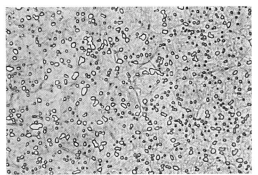

For comparison, here is the microstructure of a hardened 12C27 steel from Sandvik. Here, too, the carbides are embedded, but they are much smaller and relatively equally distributed.

chemical composition. Unalloyed carbon steel with a carbon content of less than 0.78 percent forms no carbides when tempered. This makes possible the finest cutting edges. Higher-alloyed steels must contain carbides, which should not be too large and must be well embedded in the surrounding steel structure. Only then do the resulting protective effect and reduction of wear come into effect. That requires a larger cutting angle and thus comes at a cost in maximum blade sharpness.

Chapter Summary

From iron ore mined from the ore deposits of this world, steelworks produce steel. Carbon is first added to the iron, turning it into steel. With the addition of other alloying elements such as chromium, manganese, tungsten, vanadium, and niobium, engineers create hundreds of types of steel, all of which have certain characteristics.

Steel is the body and heart of a true knife. At present there is no material that brings with it so many desirable qualities. Knife makers and smiths reshape steel by hammering or grinding and give it a knife shape.

So that the steel can be used for cutting for a long time, it must be tempered. The steel undergoes a defined temperature treatment, bringing out its potential worth and determining whether the steel will be hard, durable, or brittle. The appropriate steps are heating to a certain temperature, the subsequent abrupt cooling, and then several gentle warming phases.

Steels can be classified by the way they are made (usually furnace vs. powder-metallurgical production) by the proportion of alloying elements, and also by the degree of corrosion resistance (rust-resistant vs. non-rust-resistant).

TRIVIA: ALLOYING ELEMENTS: How They Work

In the simplest case, steel consists of iron (Fe) and the alloying element carbon (C). As simple as this combination is, it is also good. By adding small amounts of other alloying tank elements, the qualities of the steel (e.g., its corrosion resistance) can be improved. The alloying elements create certain effects in the steel with interactions and sensible upper limits. The maxim "the more the better" does not apply to steel alloying, or at best very little.

▶ Carbon (C) is the most important alloying element: its addition in quantities from 0.3 to 2 percent turn iron into steel. Steel becomes temperable from a carbon concentration of at least 0.3 percent. While the steel's strength and temperability rise with an increased carbon content, flexibility, malleability, weldability, and toughness diminish.

▶ Cobalt (Co) forms small carbides but improves high-temperature strength and refines the microstructure of the steel. It is used for so-called high-speed steel, which is used for tools exposed to high temperatures.

▶ Chromium (Cr) is an important alloying element. From 10.5 percent chromium in the basic mass, a steel is considered rustproof. With carbon, iron, tungsten, and molybdenum, chromium forms hard (mixed) carbides that improve wear resistance.

▶ Manganese (Mn) is considered an alloying element only at or above 0.5 percent. It improves temperability, strength, and a steel's forgeability and weldability.

▶ Molybdenum (Mo) forms very hard carbides, improves hardenability, increases corrosion resistance, and reduces brittleness.

▶ Niobium (Nb) is a powerful former of carbides and improves a steel's strength and durability. It also makes the microstructure more fine grained.

▶ Nickel (Ni) combined with chromium increases corrosion resistance. It is used mainly in rustproof stainless steels.

▶ Phosphorus (P) is an undesirable impurity whose content must be reduced as much as possible.

▶ Sulfur (S) also appears mainly as an impurity. It is used in some kinds of steel to improve workability.

▶ Silicon (Si) is considered an alloying element only at 0.5 percent or higher and has a positive effect on flexural strength and wear resistance. It is a typical alloying element for spring steels.

▶ Vanadium (V) and tungsten (W) form very hard carbides. Both alloying elements are used for tool steels that are exposed to high mechanical loads.

Powder-metallurgical-produced steels (here Damast steel on a hunting knife by Heiner Schmidbauer) have a finer microstructure than usual smelted steel with the same alloying elements.

Damascus steel consists of various types of steel that are initially coated in layers and subsequently joined together through heat and reshaping.

Among the most important characteristics of blade steel are achievable hardness, the degree of wear resistance, durability, the fineness of the microscopic structure, and rust resistance. Several of these parameters are in a conflict of objectives. Especially hard and wear-resistant steels are not all that durable and are consequently likely to break. Steels with an especially fine microscopic structure are as a rule highly resistant to mechanical stresses and can be finely ground, but they can rust and are not as wear resistant. As so often in life, one must find a suitable compromise.

Chapter 12. Sharpening Knives Properly: Sharpness in Focus

Have you ever been at a market and remained standing, fascinated, at a knife-sharpening stand? Where the merchant loudly advertises his grinding stones, and to prove it to the market visitors he quickly makes the knife so sharp that it turns the test paper strip into confetti. Is knife sharpening really so simple?

Well almost . . . The grinding stone salesman has a feel for the knife they give him, and of course knows precisely what he must do: with his coarse and effective abrasives he is able to quickly give the knives a grind that is sufficient to cut paper.

This looks impressive and, for the majority of knife owners, may mean an entirely new experience in knife sharpness.

But for high-grade cutting tools it must be more precise and finer. One can make it into a science—but one does not have to. Whether one sharpens the blade with a rough grinding stone or a carefully soaked Japanese waterstone, the objective is the same: the cutting bevels must come together and, in doing so, form a reasonably thin edge. To do so one must remove steel.

TRIVIA: SHARPNESS: Realization of a President

At the start of his political career, Abraham Lincoln still earned money as a wood-worker and until his violent death was a passionate carver. He had a clear opinion about the meaning of sharpness. Lincoln is claimed to have said: "Give me six hours to fell a tree, and I will spend the first four sharpening my axe."

His realization: someone with a demanding task to perform needs an efficiently formed and well-sharpened tool.

Caution, sharp! A sharp blade can be wielded under control as well as a dull one, which in turn enhances safety.

With a well-shaped and sharpened blade (here the South Fork by Spyderco), even difficult cutting tasks can be performed easily.

Dull vs. Sharp

Even a perfectly sharpened blade of the hardest steel loses its sharpness over time. The fine cutting edge is not endlessly durable: it breaks at highly stressed points, bends, wears, or is gnawed by rust—in the course of which it moves ever farther upward and spreads. And the wider a cutting edge is, the more force one must use to separate the molecular bonds of the material being cut.

When it becomes obvious that more force is required when cutting, at the latest it is time to do something. What? Grind! One must remove some material, and in doing so reshape the cutting edge. To do this one needs a sharpening medium: it must be harder (or contain harder elements) than the blade steel and also have a certain roughness (so-called grit). Large-grit abrasives remove material quickly and relatively uncontrolled, while especially fine abrasives lead to polishing and an extremely smooth surface. In the process, steel is hardly affected.

The Most-Important Sharpening Tools and Their Uses

A wide variety of abrasives are used around the world, from natural stone such as the Arkansas oil stone or the Belgian whetstone, to diamond-coated grinding stones, to silicon carbide sandpaper, synthetic Japanese waterstones, and whetstones. They differ in their grinding components, and especially the shapes in which they are offered.

Sharpening Stones

Sharpening on a stone is the supreme discipline. Why? Quite simple: whoever masters freehanded grinding on the stone is independent and in an emergency can even sharpen his knife on a flat river pebble (which typically contains hard minerals).

Japanese waterstones: Waterstones are called such because before grinding they must be soaked in water and repeatedly wetted during grinding. Japanese waterstones come in every conceivable grit. Values from 60 to 800 designate coarse stones used for repairs, or to regrind the geometry. Grits of 800 to 2,000 are used to grind blades that, while dull, are still intact. The fine grind and polishing are accomplished using grits of 2,000 to 10,000.

There are natural stones obtained in quarries and synthetically manufactured waterstones. High-quality natural stones are luxury items, since they are very rare and expensive. Even today, in Japan the finest stones are used for polishing swords. Natural grinding stones often contain garnet particles (silicon) or embedded corundum as abrasive grains. In artificially made waterstones, granules of aluminum oxide, silicon carbide, or chromium oxide are used. These stones are consistently permeated with these abrasive grain particles.

Natural stones, or ones with stones bound by synthetic resin, are softer and wear down more quickly than ceramically bound stones, which wear more slowly. There are

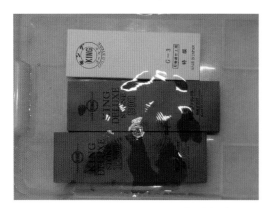

Japanese waterstones are soaked before use, filling the porous material. They are kept damp during sharpening.

The Belgian whetstone is a natural stone that is mounted on a base. It is effective thanks to its fine microstructure and good feedback.

Arkansas grinding stone contains quartz and granite abrasive grains. It is usually used with oil and not water. *RH Preyda Co.*

Diamond sharpening stones come in a variety of grits and qualities. Manufacturer DMT (here the Duo Sharp model) has a good reputation. *DMT*

advantages and disadvantages of the softer bonding: as a result of the rapid abrasion, new abrasive particles are constantly released, and the detached particles act like an abrasive paste. The abrasion progresses more rapidly on softer-bound grinding stones than on ones with harder bonds. Softer bonds are recommended for especially hard and wearproof steels and rather harder bonds for normal steels.

Belgian whetstones: These stones are mined in the Belgian Ardennes. The sedimentary rock was created from volcanic ash and clay about 480 million years ago and contains high concentrations of relatively small, faceted garnet with diameters between 0.005 and 0.02 mm. Belgian whetstones are used with water and are best suited for fine grind. Their sharpening characteristics are equivalent to Japanese waterstones with grits from 600 to 2,500.

Arkansas oil stones: Arkansas or Washita stones are designations for novaculite. This fine-grained flint is very brittle, hard, and dimensionally stable, and its abrasive grains are quartz and granite. Before grinding, novaculite is treated with thin, acid-free oil or petroleum. Novaculite is mined in the US, mainly in Arkansas and Oklahoma. The original inhabitants of North America used the stone for arrowheads and spearpoints.

Ceramic grinding stones: Most synthetic grinding stones and sharpeners (such as the Spyderco Sharpmaker) are made of aluminum oxide compounds (corundum). Red-colored corundum is also called "synthetic ruby" in the trade. Ceramic grinding stones are used dry, are very hard, and are available in many different grits.

Diamond-coated grinding stones: Diamond is the hardest known material and is therefore also used for grinding. High-grade diamond grinding stones consist of aluminum or steel blocks coated with a diamond granulate (in a carrier substance). They range from very fine to coarse. The initially high aggressiveness in removing material evens out after some time. Good diamond-coated grinding stones last a very long time if they are used carefully: one grinds with light pressure; otherwise the grains break out of the thin coating. Diamond sharpeners can be used dry or with water.

Sharpening Steel or Sharpening Block

As a rule, a sharpening steel consists of a handle and a rod of very hard steel. This can be hard chromium plated, causing the surface of the rod to be even harder. Also typical is a certain roughness of the rod, which depending on the model can be very coarse.

Similar in shape are ceramic knife sharpeners, whose sharpening block consists of aluminum oxide. They range in price from cheap to relatively expensive. Examples costing just a few dollars—for example, from a well-known Swedish furniture house—are thinner and not always finely made. At the upper end are sharpening blocks such as the Sieger Longknife, with its reddish aluminum oxide (synthetic ruby) rod, which is highly recommended.

The Sieger Longlife sharpening rod (*top*) produces fast and good results for sharpness. It is as suitable for cooking knives as it is for folding or other knives with smooth cutting edges.

Even beginners can have sharp knives with sharpening devices such as the Spyderco Sharpmaker. Here the sharpening angle is set by anchoring the triangular rods in the base plate.

When working with sharpening steel, it is always the blade and not the steel that is moved. You can hold the steel in front of yourself and then draw the blade across it—once away from yourself and then back again. You can also place the steel vertically on the table in front of you and let the blade slide down, right, and then left at the desired angle. One can also hold the steel at an angle and move the knife downward in a vertical line.

Important things to remember when sharpening with a steel are to place the blade on it as gently as possible, to maintain the angle, and not to exert too much pressure. This is also true of all other sharpening methods. Basically one always works against the cutting edge, not with it! This is true for all sharpening methods, with one exception: only when pulling a straight razor across a leather strop does the edge trail.

Sharpening Devices

Sharpening devices are designed so that one can achieve a good result without great prior knowledge and manual abilities.

Hard metal and grinding roller sharpeners: In do-it-yourself stores, furniture stores, and cutlery dealers, you often see tools that you can place on a table and then pull the blade through a slot. This sounds simple, and it is. It is in fact as easy as child's play.

The grinding work is done by grinding inserts positioned with a certain angle between them and that one rolls the blade past at a specified angle. On many of these quick sharpeners, the inserts are made of hard metal, which can lead to a very large removal of material. With a grinding roller sharpener, one pulls the knife through a slot, putting the ceramic rollers in motion, which remove material from both sides of the blade.

If these devices are not finely adjusted or are equipped with overly aggressive grinding inserts, one ends up with a very coarse blade. There are high-grade systems, but even these are limited in their range of applications.

Vee sharpeners and sharpening devices with sharpening-stone guide: Vee sharpeners usually consist of a base frame and grinding rods of various grits. The Sharpmaker made by American company Spyderco is one of the best-known devices of this type. The basic version consists of a base plate and two pairs of grinding rods made of aluminum oxide ceramic. The dark rods remove a medium amount of material and are suitable for sharpening. The white rods are finer and remove only a little material. They are suitable for maintaining sharpness or for smoothing a cutting edge.

The rods can be anchored in the base so that they are separated by a 30- or 40-degree angle. The resulting grind angle of 15 or 20 degrees is suitable for almost all knives and purposes. Its use is quite simple: all one must do is guide the blade along the rods in a downward motion. Even serrated blades and inward curved blades can be sharpened with it. In addition to the basic equipment, there are especially fine grinding rods and diamond and boron

TRIVIA: GRIT: It Must Be Rough

An abrasive's grit indicates the size of the abrasive grains being used. Basically the larger the number of the grit, the smaller the abrasive grains and the finer the removal of material and the grind. The European standards (FEPA P for sandpaper and FEPA F for grinding stones) and the Japanese standards (JIS) are based on different units of measurement and are not directly comparable.

A P500 sandpaper is roughly equivalent to an F320 grit on European grinding stones and a J600 grit in Japan. Put another way: the abrasive particles for these values have a diameter of 0.03 millimeters; 1500 sandpaper, on the other hand, is equivalent to a 500 grit on a European grinding stone and a 1200 grit on a Japanese one (or rather, an abrasive grain diameter of 0.013 millimeters).

nitride grinding rods that are very effective in removing material.

As an alternative there are several sharpeners in which the knife is fixed in a clamping or screwing device and the grinding stones are moved. The grind angle can be set in a large variety of positions. Especially large blades must be clasped during sharpening. Among the best-known makers of this kind of sharpener are Lansky and Wicked Edge. Because of their well-thought-out and high-grade grinding-stone composition and their solid design, these sharpeners can also provide good results without special knowledge.

Makeshift Sharpeners

For those on a budget, blades can also be sharpened with household materials. It is no fairy tale that knives were once pulled across the bottoms of unglazed porcelain plates to sharpen them. Among other things, porcelain contains quartz, with an abrasive effect. It can be recommended only in an emergency—or for fun.

Very good results can be achieved with wet/dry sandpaper and emery cloth. The carrier material for the abrasive usually has hard silicon carbide particles glued to it. To achieve a flat support surface, wet a sheet of glass with water and lay the sandpaper on it—it literally sucks down onto the glass. One can also stretch the sandpaper over a book or even place it on one's thigh. Sandpaper is available in a wide range of grits.

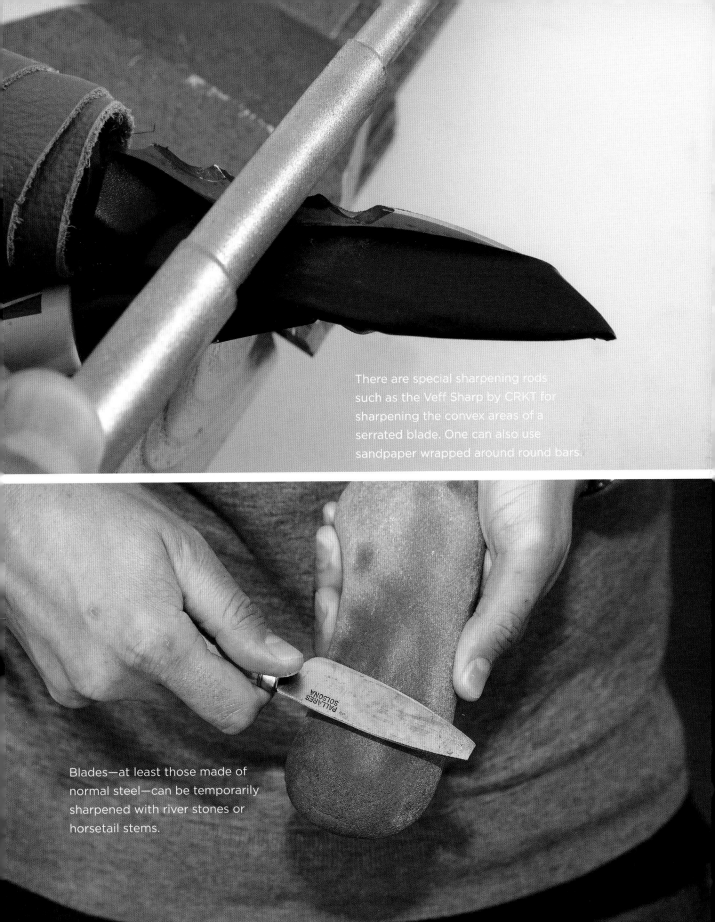

There are special sharpening rods such as the Veff Sharp by CRKT for sharpening the convex areas of a serrated blade. One can also use sandpaper wrapped around round bars.

Blades—at least those made of normal steel—can be temporarily sharpened with river stones or horsetail stems.

Even the much-talked-about river pebble can be used for the temporary sharpening of knives, since they frequently consist of hard quartz grains. Even wear-resistant steels can be sharpened this way. Afterward, one should again indulge the blade with a professional grinding stone.

Tips from the Pros
for Beginning Knife Sharpeners

The time for sharpening is reached, at the latest, when one becomes dissatisfied with a knife's cutting performance. One must not wait so long that blade wear reaches the stage when its performance is noticeably diminished. Professionals keep their knives in good condition at all times. Thus, one always has a sharp blade and also takes care of it.

If a blade is really dull, one must remove a lot of material with coarse abrasives. To maintain sharpness, a fine-grit grinding stone is sufficient, with which one can remove very little material in a controlled way. The time required to maintain sharpness is also minimal. A few passes over a grinding stone or whetstone suffices for regular maintenance.

Don't Worry
about the Right Angle

The greatest worry for sharpening novices is the constant sharpening angle one is supposed to maintain. In the beginning, not everyone can correctly estimate how far one must lift the blade spine to grind the blade at an angle of 15, 17, or 20 degrees (or whatever angle is desired). And even if one could do so, one still must execute the sharpening movement so that the angle remains constant.

But one really does not need to have fear of freehand sharpening. First practice sharpening with suitable knives and an inexpensive beginner's sharpening set, such as the one made by German manufacturer Zische. You can saw brackets from wood to check the grind angle with. To determine the sharpening angle, place a protractor on the stone.

Alternately one can calculate the distance the blade spine should be from the grinding stone by using the following formula: the width of the blade is divided by 3, 4, 5, or 6. The result equates to the distance between the grinding stone and the knife spine for the grinding angles 20, 15, 12, or 10 degrees (in this sequence).

For a sharpening angle of 20 degrees, a 1.2-inch-wide blade must be raised until the spine is 0.4 inches above the grinding stone (30 divided by 3). To grind the same blade at 15 degrees, lift the blade until the height above the grinding stone is 0.3 inches (30 divided by 4).

It can also be done by feel: place the blade flat on the grinding stone. Gradually lift the spine, make a sharpening movement, and sense the moment when the edge just

To properly resharpen a Scandinavian knife, one must position the blade so that the entire cutting bevel (here there is no secondary bevel) makes contact.

Many people shy away from sharpening because the first step—finding the correct setting angle—discourages them. Self-made angle aids make the beginning easy.

begins to engage the grinding stone. That would be the correct angle to sharpen the blade geometry of the knife in question. Or imagine that you want to remove a fine shaving—this also usually works very well. Experienced knife sharpeners hear when the blade is in the right position.

The Marker Trick

On blades with a secondary bevel, which is typical of most flat- and hollow-grind blades, the area to be ground is seldom wider than 0.08 of an inch. The cutting bevels are usually easily to recognize. As an aid, mark them from beginning to end with a permanent marker. Allow the color to dry

TRIVIA: THE CORRECT SHARPENING ANGLE: With Help from a Computer

Anyone with access to a spreadsheet application such as Excel and who knows the width of his blade and at which angle he wishes to grind can determine exactly how far he must raise the blade spine to achieve it.

Create the following three fields: sharpening angle in degrees (half the sharpening angle if both sides are to be ground), blade height in millimeters (distance between the cutting edge and spine), and distance in millimeters (distance to be maintained between the grinding stone and the blade spine). Each of these fields has a clear allocation in the form of letters (column) and numbers (row). Use the last field with the following function (only the letters and numbers of the fields are entered): =SIN(field_sharpeningangle/360*2*PI())*$column_bladeheight$row_bladeheight

C2		=SIN(field_sharpeningangle/360*2*PI())
	A	B	C
1	**Sharpening angle in degrees**	**blade height in mm**	**distance in mm between grinding stone and blade longitudinal axis**
2	40	25	16,0696902422

The marker trick helps in recognizing and maintaining the correct sharpening angle. The cutting edge is marked. If the marking is completely rubbed off, one is sharpening at the correct angle.

If one is not successful at sharpening, one is perhaps using too fine an abrasive. Scythe whetstones and coarse grinding stones (here from Zische) are rough and remove material rapidly.

briefly. Then begin grinding. When the color is completely wiped off to the cutting edge, one has the right angle. If the color is removed only from the lowest edge, then the spine is slightly too high. If grinding removes only the upper part of the marking, then you are holding the blade too flat.

In the beginning this trick is very helpful. As a beginner, one should continue marking the cutting bevels from time to time. One can thus be sure that one is grinding at the right angle. With time, one gets a feeling for the right angle. If you have no marker in the house, use a powerful magnifying glass to examine the marks left by grinding. Sharpen until the blade is again sharp or a burr is formed.

The Burr

"The burr is your friend," say experienced knife sharpeners. This "friend" is a thin, scarcely visible, but usually palpable metal ridge. It is created during sharpening, when one has "driven" one cutting bevel so far that it meets the other cutting bevel and protrudes there. The burr raises itself toward the side opposite the bevel that has been ground. The tip of the thumb is ideally suited for feeling the burr.

During sharpening, one repeatedly feels to determine if a burr has formed. If this is the case on the entire length, sharpen the other side of the bevel until the burr has moved completely to the other side; this usually does not take too long. This is the time to switch to the next sharpening stone grit.

The burr should be removed before doing so. To do so, one can guide the blade's cutting bevels along the stone, continually changing sides, once again with no pressure. Ten to twenty strokes should suffice to remove the burr.

The further one progresses in sharpening and the finer the abrasives become, the smaller the burr that forms becomes. One should continue to carry out the procedure for removing the burr—even if one cannot feel it.

So much for theory, which for many also works in practice. Not all steels form a clearly perceptible burr. If there is doubt, the marker trick helps determine whether one can move to a finer grit.

In closing, another important tip: if you grind and grind a dull blade and are certain that you are also sharpening the right place at the right angle (marker method / angle formula) and the blade still does not become sharp, then take a sharpening stone with a coarse surface (lower grit). By far the greatest part of the sharpening process is accomplished by coarse-grit grinding stones. Only when the blade is perceptibly sharp should one switch to a finer grinding grit suitable for removing and polishing. Only for maintaining sharpness can one begin with a fine or even very fine grinding stone.

If thin paper is separated in a pulling knife motion with minimal pressure, the blade is sharp.

It is said that there are knife fans with no hair on their forearms. Why is this? Arm hairs literally leap away from a very sharp blade.

Standard Methods
for Determining Sharpness

Only with the eyes and a sense of touch can one determine reasonably well how sharp a blade is. Examine the cutting edge from above under good light—possibly with the aid of a magnifying glass—and turn the blade back and forth slightly. If the cutting edge is almost impossible to see, this means that it is very thin and therefore sharp.

Where a burr has formed or the cutting edge is too wide, the light will be reflected. This is an indication that further work is required.

With some experience, sharpness can also be felt. Cautiously place the tip of your thumb on the edge and push your thumb

When sharpening on a whetstone, the blade is set at the grinding angle and pushed forward. To follow the blade's curvature, pull the blade back in a similar way.

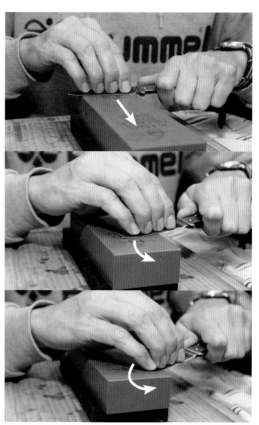

Sharpening the other side of the blade. Alternately, one can also—without changing grip—place the edge on the opposite end of the stone and pull the blade toward oneself.

TRIVIA: SHARPENING A SHAVING RAZOR:
Get Out the Leather

Stropping and sharpening shaving razors is basically quite simple. The cross section of a shaving razor is so designed that one must put down only the back edge and the cutting edge. Only these two parts of the blade make contact with the strop or the sharpening stone. The spine is not raised, since that would produce a microbevel, which is undesirable on a shaving razor.

The sharpness of a razor can be maintained for weeks to many months solely by the use of a leather strop, depending on beard growth and frequency of use. The leather of a paddle strop is highly tensioned. The leather on an untreated leather strop (possibly with a hemp sleeve on the back) is sufficient to maintain the extremely thin cutting edge. The cutting edge is pulled behind the spine and not pushed into the leather. If the leather is rubbed with sharpening paste, a minimal amount of material is removed or the blade is only polished.

Stropping is never carried out immediately after shaving, instead always prior to shaving. The reason for this is that the fine cutting edge is sometimes partly bent through contact with tough beard hairs but, after several hours, returns to its original shape. The reason for this is probably the resilience of the steel. One wishes to exploit this "self-healing"—"waiting pays off," it is also said. Therefore the waiting. This is also why men who shave daily have at least two razors.

Before shaving, strop the razor ten to twenty times per side. This is how it is done:

Tension the strop. Place the blade on it and, without applying pressure, draw the blade toward you, spine first. Turn the blade only over the spine.

The whole thing in reverse. With narrow strops, the blade moves over the width of the strop until the entire length of the blade has been stropped.

quite gently across it. This will give you an impression of how "sharp edged" the cutting edge is. Do not press on the edge from above and under no circumstances pull your thumb across it lengthwise. This can quickly lead to serious injury!

A popular method is to place the edge at an angle on the hair of the back of the head or the thumbnail. If the blade immediately "bites," it is sharp. If it slips off, it is dull. The cutting of paper (thin newspaper or cigarette paper is especially challenging) is considered proof of a cutting edge's sharpness. If one must pull to cut the paper, while the blade is sharp, it is still quite coarse and should be improved with a fine grit. If the blade cuts the paper with pressure alone (test at several places on the edge), it is sharp and well smoothed.

Another method is shaving the hair of the forearm. The English term "hair popping sharp" has not sprung from nowhere. When contacted by a really sharp blade, the hair literally "leaps" away. Attention: if the blade shaves in just one direction, this usually means that there is a burr on the blade that must be removed. Careful removal on a fine abrasive medium or a few gentle strokes with soft wood is usually effective.

Sharpening a Knife on a Whetstone

Those who are rather more interested in knives should become involved with sharpening blades. Even blades made of the hardest and most-wear-resistant steels become dull at some point. And only someone who

has mastered sharpening on a whetstone is really free. Freehand sharpening is not difficult. At least not as difficult as many think— or as many would like to believe. All that one needs is a suitable sharpening medium over which one can push the blade as constantly as possible at a suitable sharpening angle.

Whether one uses a natural Belgian stone, a whetstone with a diamond-coated surface, or a Japanese waterstone, the sharpening movements are basically the same. If the knife subsequently cuts clearly better than before, you have won. Everything else is higher art.

The following tips form a good basis but can be adapted to suit the individual. There are many ways leading to the objective. At first, practice sharpening with simple knives (such as an Opinel of nonrustproof carbon steel) that are easy to sharpen. These will be your personal entry into the subject, and the movements will become ingrained.

To begin, position the whetstone so that you can work comfortably on it. Placing it in the "twelve o'clock position" (3 two hours) works well for many.

One hand grips the handle (as a rule, the right hand for right-handers) and the other is placed on the blade. Place the thumb of this hand on the blade spine, near the handle. The index, middle, and ring fingers are positioned on the side of the blade.

If you are uncertain as to the angle to maintain, mark the cutting bevel with a marker or use an angle wedge made of paper or cardboard, a spacer, or something similar.

Concerning sharpening movement: many professionals recommend moving the blade in a cutting motion in a straight line over the whetstone. For others, a sweeping motion like a windshield wiper works better. The elbow of the handle hand acts as the fulcrum and hinge. Make the right wrist stiff and push the blade back and forth from the shoulder joint of the left arm.

If the work angle is basically correct, there will be unavoidable shaking, resulting in changes of angle without an appreciable effect. Just don't stop!

Grind with a sufficiently coarse stone until the blade feels perceptibly sharp (burr formation). In no case should you change to a finer stone; otherwise it will take much longer or achieve nothing. About 80 percent of sharpening work is done with the coarse stone.

Alternately grind one side and then the other. Five to thirty passes on one side and five to thirty on the other side produces an even removal of material on both cutting bevels and ensures a good rhythm. Here one must determine which sequences work best and produce the best results.

Changing sides: for most right-handers, grinding the left cutting bevel with a forward thrust works well. But what to do when it is the turn of the left bevel? Either (1) keep the handle in the right hand, turn the spine over, begin the sharpening movement at the far end of the whetstone, and pull the blade edge-first toward you, or (2) take the handle in your left hand, push the blade forward as before, and again have a good view of

Preparing the leather strop by oiling it with leather oil or ballistol. The skin side will later produce rather more-precise results.

On leather strops 20 x 5 centimeters or larger, add a drop of sharpening paste (here from Zische) from a tube and spread.

After two hours, finish with a spatula. Then wait another twelve hours. Thus treated, the strop is good for dozens of knives.

the height of the blade spine. Both methods work. If the blade is rounded toward the tip, then follow it, turning the handle gently as you push forward. Maintain the original work angle and do not lift the blade spine.

If the blade has become noticeably sharper or the burr-changing-sides game is behind you, it is time to turn to the fine-grit finishing stone. Repeat the grinding process until the burr forms, and complete the sharpening work with several pressureless passes over the stone, alternating sides.

If the blade is sharp, then no shiny cutting passages will be visible under a magnifying glass. If newspaper can be cut cleanly in one go, then the blade is really sharp. Cutting freaks and lovers of superclean cutting crown their work with stropping on leather.

Stropping on Leather

When stropping on leather, one has images of traditional straight razors in one's head. In fact, stropping on leather can turn the sharp blade of any knife into a hellishly sharp one, and with relatively little work.

In preparation, thin leather, which is as hard as possible and not tanned with chromium, is treated with a nonabrasive leather oil or ballistol and then rubbed with a fine polishing paste (pea-size drop). It is best to wear gloves when spreading it. By rubbing, the abrasive particles in the polishing paste (aluminum oxide, silicon carbide, diamond particles, and chromium and iron oxide) are well embedded in the leather and are present in sufficient quantities to help many

On the leather one moves the blade not against the cutting edge, but . . .

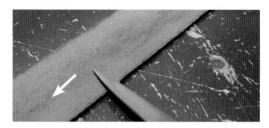

. . . with the spine forward and at a suitable sharpening angle. Work without pressure.

The other side of the blade is also pulled over the leather and not pushed.

After about ten pulling movements, the burr should be gone and the cutting edge polished.

TRIVIA: SPECIAL SHAPES: Convex and Compound Bevel

A compound bevel is a grind of the cutting bevel made up of at least two angles. It is quite popular and in some cases is supplied that way by the manufacturer, but it can easily be created afterward.

To do so, one first grinds the cutting bevel at a fine angle until it is sharp. One then corrects the whole with a somewhat coarser grind on top, which makes the cutting edge somewhat less sharp but stronger. The combination of a relatively fine 30-degree basic grind (2 x 15 degree) topped by a 40-degree grind (2 x 20) as a microbevel has proven effective. Other angle combinations are possible.

A blade ground this way is sharper than one ground exclusively with a 2 x 20 sharpening angle, since the flanks of the blade just above the edge move closer together. At the same time, it is stronger than a cutting edge ground with a 2 x 15 sharpening angle.

The cutting bevel can also be convex, meaning that the cutting bevels do not come together in a straight line but instead are bulged outward. There is a good trick for sharpening knives ground this way: the mouse pad method. Instead of a sharpening stone, one takes wet/dry sandpaper of the correct grit and places it on a soft, yielding base. Mouse pads or sponge rubber pads are ideal.

One pushes the blade with little pressure and spine first over the base, like stropping on leather. Because of the soft base, even when pressing softly the sandpaper adapts to the curved blade shape and conforms to it. Better to hold the knife a little too flat than too steep; otherwise the cutting edge will too easily lose its roundness.

knives (up to forty) to the highest level of sharpness.

Allow this mixture to rest for twelve hours. Then rub the sharpening paste again, deeply, with a flat spatula, pulling it over the leather at a very flat angle. Then wait another twelve hours until everything is fixed, then stropping can begin.

To strop, one pulls the blade, spine forward, over the leather at a suitable angle with no pressure, polishing first one cutting bevel and then the other. A few strokes (total of ten to twenty) should suffice to remove any possible burr and polish the cutting edge. At the end of each pass, raise the knife high or turn it over the blade spine to the other side. Avoid contact between the cutting edge and the leather. This can ruin the sharpness just achieved and also damage the belt. For the same reason, also do not push the blade against the edge over the leather: you can too easily cut into the leather and ruin the belt.

Chapter Summary

The significant feature of any knife is its sharpness. But sharpness is a delicate property: even the sharpest blade of the best steel at some point loses its sharpness under use.

In the best case the cutting edge is only a few thousandths of a millimeter thick. With it, one pushes into the material being cut. Depending on the material, this can represent a heavy load on the cutting edge.

Porcelain, for example, is harder than steel and an absolute "sharpness killer." Packaging and types of rope such as sisal have the hardest mineral combinations in their structure, which have an abrasive effect. The sand-encrusted bristles of wild boars have caused many hunting knives to quickly lose their sharpness.

Cutting loads can bend the foremost area of the cutting edge, putting an end to sharpness. Under various loads, the smallest steel particles or entire carbides are removed or torn out of the cutting edge. This causes the cutting edge to become increasingly rough and gradually move upward. When it reaches a certain degree of roughness and thickness, it is dull.

But the great thing about steel—still the number one knife blade material—is that it can be resharpened. For a long time, humans have used natural smooth stones for this. Natural whetstones often contain very hard granite particles (silicon) or embedded corundum as abrasive grains. In artificially made grinding stones, granulates of aluminum oxide, silicon carbide, or chromium oxide are used. Thanks to the hardness of these particles, the cutting edge can be reshaped by the controlled removal of a small amount of material. That is what sharpening is about.

Sharpening on a whetstone or with leather is not sorcery, and with a little practice enough can be learned to make a knife sharp enough for use again. The most-important

The cutting ability of a knife is the result of the blade steel and its tempering, the blade cross section, and the sharpness. The Nilte Raggio comes very sharp from the factory.

elements, in addition to a good whetstone, are patience, calm, and a suitable motion cycle, which must be practiced a little.

There is a formula for calculating the work angle. One can also fabricate angle templates. Experienced knife sharpeners can determine by hearing and feel if the sharpening angle is correct. Then all one has to do is push the blade over the whetstone.

Meanwhile, in addition to sharpening stones there are also sharpening devices that simplify sharpening. Especially popular are the Sharpmaker vee sharpener from Spyderco, which with its two angle settings covers a wide spectrum, and guided grinding stone systems from companies such as Lansky and Wicked Edge.

Glossary: The Most-Important Terms from the World of Knives

AISI: Numbering system for types of steel from the American Iron and Steel Institute.

Alloy: The alloy indicates the components of the steel and their concentrations. Alloying and tempering determine the characteristics of different types of steel.

Arc lock: Variant of the axis lock principle developed by SOG. Unlike the axis lock, it uses a pivotal block to lock the blade in place.

Assisted opener: A semiautomatic spring mechanism on a folding knife. The blade must first be moved a small distance out of the handle manually before a spring takes over and moves the blade into the extended position.

Axis lock: A locking system developed by the manufacturer Benchmade, in which a spring-tensioned bar slides back and forth on a track cut into the handle of the knife. The butt of each blade with an axis lock has a flat spot that allows a spring-tensioned bar to lock in place when the blade is opened.

Back lock (also lock back): A widely used and proven locking mechanism for folding knives. When the knife is opened, the spine locks into a notch on the back of the blade. To close the knife, one pushes down on the exposed part of the spine to pop up the part in contact with the blade.

Ball-bearing lock: Spyderco locking mechanism in which a steel ball bearing is wedged between a fixed anvil and the blade tang

Bead blasting: Bead blasting is a nonreflective finish created by blasting the surface of a blade with various media—usually beads or sand—producing a rougher surface more prone to surface corrosion.

Besh wedge: Special type of blade grind developed by Brent Beshara, with diagonally opposed bevels converging to create a third bevel edge

Bird and trout knife: Compact knife with a slender and not-too-long blade designed for finer cutting tasks, especially for cleaning fish, birds, and small game

Blackwash finish: A surface treatment for blades and metal handles: first a dark hard-metal coating is applied (alternately, dark acid etched). The metal parts are subsequently stonewashed.

Blade launcher: A manual opening mechanism for certain models of knife. A flipper-type design forces the blade out of the handle.

Burnishing: A method of blackening low-carbon steel. The steel is bathed in a highly concentrated, boiling alkaline oxidizing salt solution, causing an iron oxide (Iron III Oxide) to form whose shade of black depends on the quality of material, the surface preparation, and the type and condition of the burnishing bath. The procedure is used to give components an attractive appearance and improve corrosion resistance.

Button lock: On a button lock knife the blade is arrested by a crossbolt of different thicknesses. To release the lock, the bolt is pushed from the outside until the thick part no longer engages the root of the blade.

Caping knife: A compact knife with a short, curved blade designed for hunting-related cutting tasks

Carbide: Carbides (such as chromium or vanadium carbide) are extremely hard carbon compounds in steel. These microscopically small granules are responsible for increased wear resistance of the steel. Their size and distribution depend on the alloying, but also on tempering and manufacturing methods. For knife blade steel, it is advantageous if the carbides are as small and equally distributed as possible. To be anchored stably enough, the carbides, regardless of their size, must be surrounded by sufficient "flesh" (steel matrix). Using a steel with large carbides, it is possible to achieve very small cutting angles. Such blades cannot be made as sharp as those made from low-alloy steels with small carbides.

Cerakote coating: Cerakote (from NIC Industries) is a ceramic-based coating used in many fields (e.g., firearms, motorsport). It provides outstanding rust protection, excellent wear resistance, hardness, and durability, and its wear resistance is claimed to be 60 percent superior to that of Teflon.

Clip: As a rule, a metal strip or bracket mounted on the handle of a knife. The clip allows the knife to be attached to a trouser pocket or belt. Spyderco was the first to produce it in quantity. Some sheaths for fixed knives are also fitted with a clip.

Composite Blade: Kershaw designation for knife blades made of two puzzle-like pieces and joined by brazing

Compression lock: A locking mechanism developed by Spyderco, which in principle acts like a reversed liner lock. The movable liner is in the top of the handle instead of the bottom.

Concealex: Heat-moldable plastic such as Kydex used by Cold Steel

Cordura: A fabric made of nylon fibers, which like many other synthetic materials comes from the American company DuPont. Its melting temperature is 210°C (410ºF). The nylon fibers are cut, newly spun, and then interwoven. The result is a tear-resistant, very heavy-duty fabric that is also widely used in the outdoor and motorcycle industries.

Convex grind: The flanks of the blade are rounded instead of straight, with a degree of outward bulge. Frequently only the cutting area is convex. The convex grind is sturdier and less likely to wedge, which is why it is often found on chopping knives and hatchets.

DLC coating: DLC is the abbreviation of diamond-like carbon. This very hard carbon coating protects against wear and corrosion and improves friction characteristics. The edges of almost all razor blades are coated with it, but also knife blades and racing car engines.

Double action: A folding knife whose blade can be opened manually or automatically (e.g., by push button) is called a double-action knife.

E-Lock: The designation used by CRKT for a knife and locking mechanism that uses a stainless-steel rocker bar for lockup. The rocker bar has a strong spring that prevents accidental release, and it can be disengaged with one hand by pressing down firmly at just the right point. Developed by designer Allen Elishewitz.

Elastomer: Elastomers are polymers both with viscosity and elasticity, such as polyurethane. The elastomers group distinguishes itself in being easily stretched and bent and returning unaided to their original shapes. They are macromolecules joined by just a few chemical bridges.

False edge: Ground but not sharpened area on the blade spine. As a rule, it begins at the point and extends for several centimeters. It makes the point finer and the blade is better suited for stabbing.

Fixed: Short form of fixed-blade knife, the name of a knife with a fixed blade

Flat grind: The blade is ground from the spine or a lower starting point at a constant angle (primary bevel). The blade flanks are flat (straight?). The actual cutting edge (secondary bevel) begins below this grind: it can also be flat (at a more obtuse angle than the grind) or bulged. A flat grind can also be ground to the cutting edge. In this case the flat grind is carried through to the cutting edge without a secondary bevel.

Flat tang: See **Tang**

Fire-safe: Safety mechanism for semiautomatic knives (assisted opener) made by Columbia River Knife and Tool. A button in the thumb stud must be pressed to open the blade.

Flipper: An assisted-opening knife is a type of folding knife that uses an internal mechanism to finish the opening of the blade once the user has partially opened it by using a flipper or thumb stud attached to the blade. With the blade extended, the flipper serves as hand protection. First used by American knife maker Kit Carson.

Folder: Short form of folding knife

Frame lock: A variant of the liner lock mechanism. Here the movable liner for locking the blade is an integral part of the handle, which is made of steel or titanium. This variant was made popular by knife maker and semicustom manufacturer Chris Reeve (on the Sebenza model), using the name Integral Lock.

Friction folder: On friction-folding knives the opening and closing of the blade is restricted only by the handle's friction against the tang; there is no spring or other locking mechanism. The French Piemontais and the Japanese *higonokami* are examples of this type of knife.

Front Lock: Designation used by manufacturer A1 Mar for a back lock mechanism with especially short locking tappet (see more under **Back lock**).

Full Tang: See **Tang**

Glide lock: Locking system by Barry Gallagher. To open, slide the bolster out, creating a tang to rotate the blade open. Slide the bolster back and the blade is locked in place.

Guard: Positioned at right angles between the blade and the handle, the guard prevents the hand from slipping onto the blade. It can be present on both sides or only on the bottom. The term has its origins in bladed weapons.

Guillochage: An old form of craftsmanship dedicated to the decoration of clocks, jewels, and also knives. Using files and other tools, decorative designs are carved into the visible parts of the back spring and scales. At some French and Italian manufacturers, every knife maker has his own design, similar to a signature.

Guthook: Belly opener on a gutting blade; also used to describe the blade as a whole. Originally designed for cutting open the belly of a wild animal. The same feature is now a part of many rescue knives, where it is used as a rope cutter.

Half stop: A feature of folding knives that is designed to enhance safety: the blade locks at an extension angle of 90 degrees. This is produced by a right-angle-shaped tang or a recess in the tang, in which the back spring engages. A certain amount of resistance must be overcome to fully extend or close the blade.

Hollow grind: On a hollow-ground blade the sides of the blade are concave instead of flat. The grind is achieved with round grinding stones or the contact wheel of a belt grinder, with the diameter of the grinding tool determining how concave the grind is. The larger the diameter of the stone or contact wheel, the closer the hollow grind approaches a flat grind.

Hytrel: DuPont brand name for thermoplastic polymer elastomers with great elasticity, tensile strength, and impact resistance over a temperature range from -40°C to +110°C (-104°F to +230°F).

Integral knife: Designation for a fixed knife in which the blade, tang, and scales are produced three-dimensionally from a single piece (milled or forged). If bolsters are present at the front and rear of the handle, then it is called a fully integral knife, whereas a knife with only a front bolster or guard is called a half-integral knife.

Integral lock: See **Frame lock**

Interlock: A blade-locking mechanism developed by Wilfried Gorski. The patent locking system is operated by a small slider in the spine of the handle. It is unlocked by pulling back against spring pressure.

Kalgard: English company specializing in coatings and lubricants. Manufacturer of polymer-based coatings for knife blades.

Kevlar: A synthetic fiber made of polyamides developed by DuPont in 1965. Kevlar fibers are very strong; have a high impact strength, high elongation, good vibration damping, and resistance to acids and alkaline solutions; and are also very heat and fire resistant. Kevlar does not melt at high temperatures; instead it begins to carbonize at 400°C (932ºF). Kevlar is best known for its use in bulletproof vests.

Kick start: An automatic spring mechanism developed by SOG Knives. A lengthwise bar in the handle blocks the blade. If the bar is pulled back, a spring extends the blade.

Kydex: A hard synthetic material consisting of an acrylic/PVC combination. The material can be heated and reshaped into a new form, which is retained when the material cools. Kydex is light, scratch, and shock resistant; flame retarding; and chemical resistant and is excellently suited for making knife sheaths.

Laminate steel: Laminated steel makes it possible to use highly tempered or nonrust-proof steel as the central cutting core. The hard central core is protected against corrosion, high-impact loads, and bending loads by softer outer layers.

Lanyard: The safety line designed to prevent loss of a knife. It is usually attached to a knife by means of a hole in the handle or a bracket.

LAWKS: Lake And Walker Knife Safety, a technical feature of knives made by CRKT. The movable liner of a liner lock knife is blocked by a pivoting lever, further securing the blade. On the Auto LAWKS version this safety is automatic, compared to the manual operation of the original version.

Lever lock: A locking system typically used in traditional switchblade knives. A flat spring mounted on the side of the handle presses the locking bolt into the blade tang (when the blade is folded or extended). A folding lever raises the spring—and with it the locking bolt—and releases the blade lock.

Levitator: A locking system developed by Benchmade that works with a side-mounted pivot lever that engages the extended or folded blade.

Liner: Metal frames of a folding knife. As a rule, two liners form the supporting handle frame, onto which plates and scales of various materials are installed. Traditionally the liners are made of brass or nickel silver, whereas on modern designs they are made of stainless steel, aluminum, or titanium.

Liner lock: A locking mechanism developed by handmade Custom Knives, which in its current form was developed by American knife maker Michael Walker. The liner lock functions with one section of the liner angled inward toward the inside of the knife. From there, it can go back to its previous position only with manual force, therefore locking it in place. The tail of the liner lock, which is closest to the blade, is cut to engage the bottom of the blade under the pivot. To disengage the lock, the user must move the liner to the side—usually with the thumb—away from the blade bottom.

Merc Harness: CRKT company designation for a simple shoulder carriage system for knives

Microscopic structure: The individual composition of the steel from iron, carbon, and possibly other alloying elements such as chromium determines its microscopic structure. The shape of the microscopic structure can be controlled by tempering. The microscopic structure affects mechanical characteristics such as hardness, wear resistance, resilience, maximum sharpness, corrosion resistance, and sharpenability.

Mid-Lock: Benchmade designation for a back lock mechanism with a short tappet. Synonymous with front lock.

Mono-Lock: Benchmade designation for a liner lock in which the blocking spring is part of the handle scale (steel or titanium). Synonymous with frame lock and integral lock.

Nak-Lock: A locking mechanism developed by knife maker Seiichi Nakamura. It works in similar fashion to a liner lock, but a bolt engages the side of the blade tang. Produced in quantity by Benchmade.

Neck knife: A knife (usually a fixed knife, but a folding knife is also possible) worn around the neck, usually on a cord. Neck knives were developed primarily for water sport enthusiasts who are unable to attach a knife to their bodies.

Opening hole: The round hole in the blade was invented by Sal Glesser, founder of Spyderco, and it is a stroke of genius in the history of folding knives. The hole allows the blade to be extended with one hand and can be used both by right- and left-handers. Because the Spyderco round shape is legally protected, other manufacturers use every possible derivative.

Open frame: Folding-knife handle made like an open framework. The spine is open and the parts are joined by pins or screws. This simplifies cleaning and reduces weight.

OTF: A type of automatic knife whose blade snaps in a straight line from out of the handle (OTF stands for "out the front"). On single-action OTFs the blade must be manually unlocked to close, while on double-action OTFs, pulling back on the slider suffices.

Outburst: CRKT designation for a semiautomatic opening mechanism

Pancake sheath: A typical feature of a pancake sheath is its relatively large area. Openings for the belt are present on the sides, either at the same height or staggered (for a diagonal sit). Most pancake sheaths are made of leather.

Paracord: Trade name for a tear-resistant nylon rope that has a braided exterior and a continuous core made of several (usually seven) individual strands. Short form of parachute cord.

Pseunetic: Kershaw designator for a so-called "flipper"

PTFE coating: PTFE (polytetrafluoroethylene) is a polymer of fluorine and carbon. This material is often called Teflon—the DuPont trade name. A PTFE coating protects against rust and reduces friction. PTFE dust is not harmful in small quantities. PTFE should not be heated to temperatures in excess of 200°C (392ºF) because poisonous gas is then formed.

Puzzle lock: Locking system by Bram Frank, in which the locking spring engages a specially formed recess in the blade tang (like one piece of a puzzle into another).

PVD method: The PVD (physical vapor deposition) coating method involves depositing metallic materials such as titanium nitride, titanium aluminum nitride, or titanium carbon nitride on metal bodies. Layer thicknesses are on the order of two to five thousandths of a millimeter.

Ricasso: Unground area of the blade between the cutting edge and the handle or guard

Rolling Lock: Benchmade designation for a mechanism in which a pin in the handle—arranged crossways—is pushed by spring force behind the blade tang, thus locking the blade. The pin is attached to a movable lever.

Rotoblock: This development by the Italian company Lion Steel is based in principle on the Lockbar Stabilizer from American knife maker Rick Hinderer, but functionally it is clearly improved. Both prevent an overextension of the locking part of the handle on frame lock knives when unlocking. By turning a pivoting button, or lockbar stabilizer, it essentially converts the knife into a fixed-blade knife.

Rust: Rust is iron oxide, a product of decomposition produced from iron or steel by oxidation with oxygen in the presence of water.

Rust resistant: Even so-called rust-free steels can be made to rust. There are rust-resistant steels if the basic mass contains at least 12 percent chromium, allowing a thin, chromium-rich oxide layer to form on the surface of the steel. This transparent layer protects the underlying steel from further reactions with the environment.

Sand blasting: Surface treatment with fine sand blown under high pressure onto the article. As a rule, knife blades and other components are not blasted with sand but with glass beads (see **Bead blasting**).

San mai: Japanese term for a three-layer blade structure with a hard cutting layer in the center and softer outer layers

San Mai III: Cold Steel designation for a three-layer blade steel

S.A.T.: SOG Assisted Technology—the SOG designation for the company's semiautomatic opening mechanism

Satin finish: High-grade surface preparation carried out by a polishing machine. It appears as an even structure of fine grind marks, which as a rule run at right angles to the blade's longitudinal axis. Various levels of quality are differentiated by the fineness of the polish.

Scandinavian grind: See **Flat grind**

Semiautomatic Knife: Knife with a semiautomatic opening mechanism (see **Assisted opener**)

Side lock: Folding-knife mechanism in which the blade is locked in the extended and folded positions by a spring-guided slide. This technique is used by Simbatec and Gerber.

Slipjoint: A folding-knife design variant in which the extended blade is held in position by a back spring but is not locked. Friction is the effective force.

Snap Lock: CRKT designation for a locking mechanism for knives with sideways opening blades developed by Ed Van Hoy. To open, one presses down on the front cam lever mechanism with one's thumb and rotates the blade outward until it fully extends and clicks securely into place. To close the blade, one presses down on the cam lever to disengage, then moves the blade back into the closed position. When the blade is closed, no part of the edge is exposed and the knife is safe to carry.

Speed Safe: Kershaw designation for its semiautomatic opening mechanism developed by knife designer Chris Onion, who made this type of knife popular

Spring knife: A folding knife whose blade springs from the handle when a button or lever is pushed. There are various types of spring mechanism with spiral or leaf spring.

Stonewash finish: A surface treatment in which the components are "washed" with abrasive—mainly stone-shaped abrasive bodies in a drum—resulting in a random, fine scratch pattern. This pattern conceals later signs of wear.

Stud Lock: Kershaw designation for a locking mechanism in which the action is in the blade. The double-sided thumb pin is pressed backward by a spring and engages a cutout in the handle. The pin is pressed forward to release the lock.

Suminagashi: Japanese designation for a laminated blade. A *suminagashi* blade has a central cutting layer of hard monosteel. Several layers of two different steels (Damast) are laminated on both sides.

Tactical Operation Lock: A patented locking system from Lion Steel that combines elements of the slipjoint and axis lock. A sprung cross pin locks the back spring so that it cannot be moved. If the cross pin is pulled back, the blade is held in working position only by spring pressure.

Tapered tang: Designation for a flat tang that tapers toward the end

Tail lock: A variant of the back lock mechanism in which the lock is released by pressing on the lever at the end of the handle

Tang: The extension of the blade that reaches into the handle. There are flat and round tangs. On the first, handle scales are added to both sides, while on the second, the handle is placed onto the tang and held in place by screwing, riveting, or gluing. As a rule, high-quality knives have a full tang that extends all the way through the handle.

Tek Lock: Product name of a mounting system with which a Kydex knife sheath can be attached to the belt or to equipment in several positions

Tempering: Precisely defined heating and cooling processes to influence certain features of a steel blade, such as hardness and resilience. Steel blades are often shaped in an annealed state (stamped, cut, filed) and ground. For hardening, the blade must be heated and kept at that temperature for a certain time—depending on the type of steel, between 800°C and 1,200°C (1,470°F–2,190°F). The resulting iron structure is called austenite. In the process the carbon atoms in the steel leave their original positions and in this microscopic structure arrange themselves on interstitials. If the steel is then cooled abruptly, the carbon atoms are fixed in the iron lattice. This tension ultimately produces hardness. The resulting microscopic structure is called martensite. Targeted reheating reduces the hardness tensions produced by the cooling process, and the steel becomes a little softer, but also more resilient. By subsequent deep cooling—which is frequently undertaken—the microscopic structure can be refined.

Textolite: A synthetic material made of phenol resin and various carrier materials (such as wool or glass fiber) that has been in production since the 1950s

Thermoplastic: A synthetic material whose consistency changes with temperature, allowing it to be shaped

Three-finger knife: A compact fixed knife whose handle can accommodate only three fingers (the thumb is not counted) instead of four. Analogous to this, there is also a two-finger knife.

Thumb hole: See **Opening hole**

Thumb stud: Opening aid on the blade of a folding knife to enable one-handed opening with the thumb. The stud can be on one or both sides.

Tip-up / tip-down: Ways of carrying a folding knife on the body—with the blade point ("tip") up or down. These depend on how the attachment clip is mounted on the knife—on many knives this can be changed. When carrying a knife tip up, it is important that the folded blade be safely held in the handle and not accidentally come out; otherwise the danger of injury is great.

Titanium: A light, very robust, completely rustproof, antimagnetic and antiallergenic metal that on knives is used primarily as a material for liners and scales, but sometimes for blade material. Pure titanium is normally used for handles and scales, and the spring-hard titanium alloy 6A14V for liners (especially on liner lock folding knives). Titanium has roughly the same strength as steel but is about a third lighter.

Trainer version: Practice version of a knife, with a harmless rubber or plastic blade. Practice versions of self-defense knives are used, so safely practice usage techniques.

Tri-Ad Lock: Modified back lock made by Cold Steel with a separate blade stop

Tru-Sharp: Case designation for rust-resistant 420HC steel

Tungsten carbide: This extremely hard compound is formed from the elements tungsten, carbon, and cobalt. Its uses include tool blades, ballpoint pen balls, and glass breakers.

Twin Pin Lock: Böker designation for a locking mechanism with a radially arranged pin

Two-finger knife: Compact folding knife on whose grip only two fingers can fit instead of four. Analogous to the three-finger knife.

Ultra-Lock: Cold Steel designation for a variant of the axis lock principle. As on SOG's arc lock mechanism, the locking pin behind the blade tang is on a lever.

Wave: The wave mechanism (a term coined by Emerson Knives) is a hook-shaped form at the end of a folding knife's blade spine. When the knife is pulled from the pocket, the hook catches on the edge of the pocket. As a result, further pulling fully extends the blade.

Wear resistance: Wear resistance is an indication of how well a steel resists mechanical wear. The more tempered a steel is, the more wear resistant it is. Of even greater importance is the number, size, and distribution of carbides in the steel matrix.

Wedge lock: A locking mechanism by Gerber in which a spring pushes a lengthwise bar behind the blade tang

The Ingredients in Steel

DESIGNATION	ALLOY CONSTITUENTS BY PERCENT												HRC HARDNESS
	CARBON	CHROMIUM	MOLYBDENUM	VANADIUM	SILICON	NICKEL	SULFUR	PHOSPHOROUS	MANGANESE	TUNGSTEN	COBALT	NITROGEN	
Non-Corrosion-Resistant Steel Type													
0170-6C (50100B)	0,95	0,45	–	0,20	–	–	–	–	0,45	–	–	–	57-60
100Cr6 (1.3505)	1,00	1,50	–	–	0,25	–	–	–	0,35	–	–	–	58-61
1055	0,52-0,60	–	–	–	0,30	–	0,05	0,04	0,60-0,90	–	–	–	56-58
1065	0,59-0,70	–	–	–	0,30	–	0,05	0,04	0,60-0,90	–	–	–	56-59
1075	0,60-0,80	–	–	–	0,30	–	0,05	0,04	0,60-0,90	–	–	–	57-59
1095	0,90-1,04	–	–	–	0,30	–	0,05	0,04	0,60-0,90	–	–	–	58-61
1095 Cro-Van	0,95-1,10	0,30-0,60	0,06	0,16	–	0,26	–	–	–	–	–	–	56-58
1770 (Uddeholm)	0,70	–	–	–	0,30	–	0,01	0,03	0,50	–	–	–	57-59
5160	0,55-0,65	–	–	–	0,15-0,30	–	–	0,04	0,75-1,00	–	–	–	56-59
52100	0,95-1,10	–	–	–	0,15-0,30	–	0,03	0,03	0,25-0,45	–	–	–	58-61
55Si7 (1.5026)	0,52-0,60	–	–	–	1,50-1,80	–	0,05	0,05	0,70-1,00	–	–	–	56-58
6168CrV	0,65-0,75	0,30-0,35	–	0,10-0,15	0,20	–	0,03	0,08	0,60	–	–	–	59-61
65Mn	0,62-0,70	0,30	–	–	0,17-0,37	–	–	0,02	0,90-1,20	–	–	–	52-56
75Cr1 (1.2003)	0,70-0,80	0,30-0,40	–	–	0,25-0,50	–	0,03	0,03	0,60-0,80	–	–	–	56-59
80CrV2 (1.2235)	0,75-0,85	0,40-0,70	–	0,10-0,25	0,25-0,40	–	0,03	0,03	0,30-0,50	–	–	–	57-59
A-2	0,95-1,05	4,75-5,50	0,90	1,40	0,50	0,30	–	–	1,00	–	–	–	57-61
A-6	0,70	1,00	1,35	–	0,30	–	–	–	2,00	–	–	–	57-59
Aogami 1)	1,20	0,20-0,50	–	–	0,20	–	–	–	0,30	1,00-1,50	–	–	60-63
Aogami Super Blue	1,40-1,50	0,30-0,50	0,30-0,50	0,50	0,10-0,20	–	–	0,03	0,20-0,30	2,00-2,50	–	–	61-65
C30 (Bessemer)	0,27-0,34	–	–	–	0,40	–	0,05	0,05	0,50-0,70	–	–	–	52-54
C75	0,70-0,80	–	–	–	0,15-0,35	–	0,03	0,04	0,60-0,80	–	–	–	55-58
C80W2 (1.1625)	0,75-0,85	–	–	–	0,10-0,30	–	0,03	0,03	0,10-0,35	–	–	–	57-59
Carbon V	1,05	0,45	–	0,15-0,20	0,20	–	–	0,01	0,50	–	–	–	56-59
D2 (K110)	1,55	11,30	0,80	0,80	0,30	–	–	–	0,40	–	–	–	58-61
DNH7	0,60-0,80	–	–	–	0,30	–	0,05	0,04	0,55	–	–	–	57-59
INFI M	0,60	8,00	1,40	0,50	1,00	0,30	0,01	0,02	0,40	0,10	0,03	–	56-58
K720	0,90	0,35	–	0,10	0,25	–	–	–	2,00	–	–	–	59-62
L6	0,65-0,75	0,60-1,20	0,50	0,20-0,30	0,50	1,25-2,00	0,03	0,03	0,25-0,80	–	–	–	57-59
M2	0,95-1,05	3,75-4,50	4,75-6,50	1,95-2,75	0,20-0,45	0,30	–	0,03	0,15-0,40	5,00-6,75	–	–	59-64

O-1	0,85-1,00	0,40-0,60	–	0,30	0,50	–	–	–	1,00-1,40	–	–	–	57-61
PSF27	1,55	12,00	0,75	1,00	0,40	–	–	–	0,40	–	–	0,30	60-61
Shirogami 2)	1,20	–	–	–	0,20	–	0,03	0,02	0,20	–	–	–	59-63
Sleipner (Uddeholm)	0,90	7,80	2,50	0,50	0,90	–	0,01	0,03	0,50	–	–	–	60-62
SK-5	0,90-1,00	–	0,30	–	0,30	–	–	–	–	–	–	–	57-60
SK-7	0,65-0,75	–	–	–	0,10-0,30	–	0,03	0,03	0,10-0,35	–	–	–	56-59
SRK-8	0,95-1,10	0,20-0,50	–	–	0,10-0,20	–	0,03	0,03	0,25	–	–	–	60-61
T508 Carbinox	0,50	8,00	–	–	0,30	–	0,02	0,02	0,30	–	–	–	56-58
U8 (A)	0,76-0,83	0,20	–	–	0,17-0,33	0,25	0,03	0,03	0,17-0,33	–	–	–	56-59
Vascowear	1,12	7,75	1,60	2,40	1,20	–	–	–	0,30	1,10	–	–	58-61
W-1	0,70-1,50	0,15	0,10	0,10	0,10-0,40	0,20	–	–	0,10-0,40	0,50	–	–	57-63
W-2	0,85-1,50	0,15	0,10	0,10	0,10-0,40	0,20	–	–	0,10-0,40	0,15	–	–	57-63
XC 65	0,60-0,70	–	–	–	0,10-0,30	–	0,03	0,03	0,10-0,35	–	–	–	56-59
XC 70	0,65-0,75	–	–	–	0,10-0,30	–	0,03	0,03	0,10-0,35	–	–	–	56-59
XC 75	0,70-0,80	–	–	–	0,10-0,30	–	0,03	0,03	0,10-0,35	–	–	–	56-59
XC 90	0,85-0,95	–	–	–	0,10-0,30	–	0,03	0,03	0,10-0,35	–	–	–	57-59
YHB2	1,20	0,20-0,50	–	–	0,20	–	–	–	0,30	1,25-1,75	–	–	60-63
YK-30	1,05	0,50	–	–	0,40	0,25	–	0,03	1,00	–	–	–	57-59
YXR7	0,80	5,00	5,00	1,10	–	–	–	–	–	1,10	–	–	62-65

= "Blue Paper Steel" (Hitachi) 2) "White Paper Steel" (Hitachi)

DESIGNATION	ALLOY CONSTITUENTS BY PERCENT												HRC HARDNESS
	CARBON	CHROMIUM	MOLYBDENUM	VANADIUM	SILICON	NICKEL	SULFUR	PHOSPHOROUS	MANGANESE	TUNGSTEN	COBALT	NITROGEN	
1.4034	0,45-0,50	12,50-14,50	–	–	1,00	–	0,02	0,04	1,00	–	–	–	52-55
1.4109	0,65-0,75	14,00-16,00	0,40-0,80	–	0,70	–	0,02	0,04	1,00	–	–	–	55-57
1.4110	0,48-0,60	13,00-15,00	–	0,05-0,15	1,00	–	0,02	0,04	1,00	–	–	–	54-56
1.4116	0,45-0,55	14,00-15,00	0,50-0,80	0,10-0,20	1,00	–	0,02	0,04	1,00	–	–	–	56-58
1.4125	0,95-1,20	16,00-18,00	0,40-0,80	–	1,00	–	0,02	0,04	1,00	–	–	–	58-60
154-CM	1,05	14,00	4,00	–	0,30	–	–	–	0,50	–	–	–	58-61
420 (=420 J2)	0,40-0,50	12,00-14,00	–	–	1,00	–	0,01	0,02	1,00	–	–	–	52-55
420 HC	0,50-0,70	12,00-14,00	–	–	1,00	–	0,01	0,02	1,00	–	–	–	54-56
420 MoV (5Cr15MoV)	0,45-055	14,00-16,00	0,60	0,10	0,40	–	0,01	0,03	0,30	–	–	–	55-57
425 Modified	0,40-0,55	13,50-15,00	0,60-1,00	0,10	0,80	–	0,03	0,04	0,50	–	–	–	56-58
440 A	0,60-0,75	16,00-18,00	0,75	–	1,00	–	0,03	0,04	1,00	–	–	–	55-57
440 B	0,75-0,95	16,00-18,00	0,75	–	1,00	–	0,03	0,04	1,00	–	–	–	56-59
440 C	0,95-1,20	16,00-18,00	0,75	–	1,00	–	0,03	0,04	1,00	–	–	–	58-60
440 XH	1,60	16,00	0,80	0,45	0,40	0,35	–	–	0,50	–	–	–	58-62
3Cr13	0,25-0,35	12,00-14,00	–	–	1,00	–	0,03	0,04	1,00	–	–	–	54-56
4Cr15MoV	0,35-0,45	14,00-16,00	0,20	0,12	0,50	0,20	0,01	0,03	0,30	–	–	–	55-57
5Cr13	0,45-0,55	12,00-14,00	–	–	1,00	–	0,03	0,04	1,00	–	–	–	55-57
5Cr13MoV	0,45-0,55	12,00-14,00	0,60	0,10	0,40	–	0,01	0,03	0,30	–	–	–	55-57
7Cr13	0,65-0,75	12,00-14,00	–	–	1,00	–	0,03	0,04	1,00	–	–	–	55-57
7Cr17	0,65-0,75	16,00-18,00	–	–	0,50	–	0,01	0,03	0,30	–	–	–	56-58
7Cr17MoV	0,65-0,75	16,00-18,00	0,20	0,12	0,50	0,20	0,01	0,03	0,30	–	–	–	57-59
8Cr13MoV	0,75-0,85	12,00-14,00	0,15	0,10	0,50	0,20	0,01	0,02	0,40	–	–	–	58-59
9Cr13	0,90-1,05	12,00-14,00	–	–	0,80	–	0,01	0,03	0,80	–	–	–	56-58
9Cr18	0,90-1,05	16,00-19,00	–	–	0,80	–	0,01	0,03	0,80	–	–	–	56-58
9Cr18MoV	0,90-1,05	17,00-19,00	0,75	0,10	1,00	–	0,03	0,04	0,80	–	–	–	58-60
9Cr13CoMoV	0,90-1,05	12,00-14,00	0,15	0,15	0,50	0,10	0,02	0,03	0,35	–	0,22	–	58-60
12C27	0,60	13,50	–	–	0,40	–	0,01	0,03	0,40	–	–	–	54-56
12C27 Mod.	0,52	14,50	–	–	0,40	–	0,01	0,03	0,60	–	–	–	54-56
13C26	0,65	13,00	–	–	0,40	–	0,01	0,03	0,65	–	–	–	55-57
14-4CrMo	1,05	14,00	4,00	–	0,30	–	–	–	0,50	–	–	–	58-60
14C28N	0,64	14,00	–	–	0,40	–	0,01	0,03	0,65	–	–	0,08	56-58
19C27	0,95	13,50	–	–	0,40	–	0,01	0,03	0,65	–	–	–	57-60
40X13	0,35-0,45	13,00	–	–	0,30	–	0,03	0,03	0,35	–	–	–	54-58
40X10C2M	1,05	14,00	4,00	0,20	0,50	0,60	0,03	0,03	0,50	–	–	–	57-58
65X13	0,60-0,75	13,00	0,75	–	1,00	–	0,03	0,04	1,00	–	–	–	56-58
95X18	0,95-1,00	17,00-19,00	–	–	0,80	0,60	0,03	0,03	0,80	–	–	–	58-60

	C	Cr	Mo	V	Mn	Ni	P	S	Si	W	Co	N	HRC
110X18	1,10	17,00-18,00	0,30	–	–	0,50	0,03	0,03	0,50	–	–	–	58-61
Acuto +	0,90-0,95	17,00-18,00	1,30-1,50	0,10-0,25	0,50	–	–	0,04	0,50	–	–	–	59-60
Acuto 440	1,00	17,50	1,40	0,20	0,50	–	–	–	0,50	–	–	–	59-60
A.N. 58	0,45	13,50	–	–	0,35	–	0,02	0,02	0,50	–	–	–	56-58
ATS-34	1,05	14,00	4,00	–	0,35	–	0,02	0,03	0,40	–	–	–	58-61
ATS-55	1,00	14,00	0,60	–	0,40	–	–	–	0,50	–	0,40	–	58-61
AUS-4	0,40-0,45	13,00-14,50	–	–	1,00	0,49	0,03	0,04	1,00	–	–	–	52-55
AUS-6	0,55-0,65	13,00-14,50	–	0,10-0,25	1,00	0,49	0,03	0,04	1,00	–	–	–	55-57
AUS-8	0,70-0,75	13,00-14,50	0,10-0,30	0,10-0,26	1,00	0,49	0,03	0,04	0,50	–	–	–	57-59
AUS-10	0,95-1,10	13,00-14,50	0,10-0,31	0,10-0,27	1,00	0,49	0,03	0,04	0,50	–	–	–	58-60
AUS-118	0,90-0,95	17,00-18,00	1,30-1,50	0,10-0,25	0,50	–	0,03	0,04	0,50	–	–	–	58-60
BG-42	1,15	14,50	4,00	1,20	0,30	–	–	–	0,50	–	–	–	57-60
B75P	1,10-1,20	14,0-15,0	3,80-4,20	1,00-1,50	0,30	–	–	–	0,50	–	–	–	60-61
CRB-7	1,10	14,00	2,00	1,00	0,30	–	–	–	0,40	–	–	–	58-61
Cronidur 30	0,25-0,35	14,00-16,00	0,85-1,10	–	0,10	0,50	–	–	0,10	–	–	0,30-0,50	58-60
CTS-BD1	0,90	15,50	0,30	0,10	0,37	–	–	–	0,60	–	–	–	60-64
GIN-1	0,90	15,50	0,30	–	0,37	–	0,03	0,02	0,60	–	–	–	58-60
H-1	0,15	14,00-16,00	0,50-1,50	–	3,00-4,50	6,00-8,00	0,03	0,04	2,00	–	–	0,10	54-56
LC 200 N	0,30	15,00	0,95	–	–	0,50	–	–	1,00	–	–	0,50	58-60
LV04	0,90	18,00	1,15	0,10	–	–	–	–	0,07	–	–	–	55-58
MBS-26	0,85-1,00	13,00-15,00	0,15-0,25	–	0,65	–	0,01	0,04	0,30-0,60	–	–	–	56-59
MRS-30	1,12	14,00	0,60	0,25	1,00	–	–	–	0,50	–	–	–	58-61
MVS-8	0,85	14,00	2,50	0,15	0,50	–	–	–	0,50	–	–	–	58-61
N 680	0,54	17,50	1,10	0,10	0,45	–	–	–	0,40	–	–	–	53-58
N 690	1,05	17,00	0,50	–	0,40	–	–	–	0,40	–	1,50	–	59-62
N 695	1,05	17,00	0,50	–	0,40	–	–	–	0,40	–	–	–	57-60
Niolox (SB1)*	0,80	12,70	1,10	0,90	–	–	–	–	–	–	–	–	57-62
T6MoV	0,60	14,00	0,60	0,15	k.A.	–	k.A.	k.A.	k.A.	–	–	–	56-58
Uginox MA5MV	0,56-0,55	14,00-15,00	0,50-0,80	0,10-0,20	0,50-1,00	–	0,01-0,02	0,04	1,00	–	–	–	54-56
VG-10 (V-10)	0,95-1,05	14,50-15,50	0,90-1,20	0,10-0,30	0,60	–	–	0,03	0,50	–	1,30-1,50	–	58-61
VG-1	0,95-1,05	13,00-15,00	0,20-0,40	–	–	0,25	–	–	–	–	–	–	58-61
X15-T.N.	0,40	15,50	2,00	0,30	0,20	–	–	0,02	0,40	–	–	0,20	57-60
X46Cr13 (Z40C13)	0,45-0,50	12,50-14,50	–	–	1,00	–	0,02	0,04	1,00	–	–	–	52-55
X50CrMoV15	0,45-0,55	14,00-15,00	0,50-0,80	0,10-0,20	1,00	–	0,02	0,04	1,00	–	–	–	56-58
X55CrMo14 (Mova-60)	0,48-0,60	13,00-15,00	0,50-0,80	0,10-0,20	1,00	–	0,015	0,04	1,00	–	–	–	56-58
X65Cr13	0,58-0,70	12,50-13,50	–	–	1,00	–	0,02	0,04	1,00	–	–	–	55-57
X100CrMo13	0,95-1,05	12,50-13,50	0,40-0,80	–	1,00	–	0,02	0,04	1,00	–	–	–	58-60
Z60	0,60-0,65	14,00	0,55-0,60	0,15-0,20	–	0,15	–	–	0,45	–	–	–	56-58
Z70CD15	0,70	15,00	0,75	–	1,00	–	0,03	0,04	1,00	–	–	–	55-57

DESIGNATION	ALLOY CONSTITUENTS BY PERCENT												HRC HARDNESS
	CARBON	CHROMIUM	MOLYBDENUM	VANADIUM	SILICON	NICKEL	SULFUR	PHOSPHOROUS	MANGANESE	TUNGSTEN	COBALT	NITROGEN	
Cowry X	3,00	20,00	1,00	0,30	-	-	-	-	-	-	-	-	63-64
CPM-154	1,05	14,00	4,00	-	0,30	-	-	-	0,50	-	-	-	58-61
CPM-10V	2,45	5,25	1,30	9,75	-	-	-	-	-	-	-	-	56-58
CPM-125V	3,20-3,40	14,00	2,50	11,50-12,25	0,40-0,60	0,40	0,03	0,03	0,40-0,60	0,50	0,50	0,10-0,50	59-64
CPM-15V	3,40	5,25	1,30	14,50	-	-	-	-	-	-	-	-	58-62
CPM-20CV	1,90	20,00	1,00	4,00	0,30	-	-	-	0,30	0,60	-	-	58-62
CPM-3V	0,80	7,50	1,30	2,75	-	-	-	-	-	-	-	-	55-57
CPM-9V	1,80	5,25	1,30	9,00	-	-	-	-	-	-	-	-	57-60
CPM-Cru-Wear	1,15	7,50	1,60	2,40	-	-	-	-	-	1,00	-	-	60-65
CPM-D2	1,50	12,00	1,00	1,00	0,60	0,30	-	-	0,60	-	-	-	58-61
CPM-M4	1,40	4,00	5,25	4,00	0,55	-	0,06	-	0,30	5,50	-	-	62-64
CTS-204P	1,90	20,00	1,00	4,00	0,60	-	-	-	0,30	0,65	-	-	58-62
CTS-XHP	1,60	16,00	0,80	0,40	0,40	0,30	-	-	0,50	-	-	-	60-62
Elmax Superclean	1,70	17,00	1,00	3,00	0,40	-	-	-	0,30	-	-	-	60-62
K190	2,30	12,50	1,10	4,00	0,40	-	-	-	0,40	-	-	-	60-64
K390	2,45	4,15	3,75	9,00	0,55	-	-	-	-	1,00	2,00	-	61-65
M390	1,90	20,00	1,00	4,00	0,70	-	-	-	0,30	0,60	-	-	58-61
PMC-27	0,60	13,50	-	-	0,50	-	-	-	0,50	-	-	-	54-56
RWL-34	1,05	14,00	4,00	-	0,50	-	-	-	0,50	-	-	-	58-61
SGPS	1,40	15,00	2,80	-	0,50	-	0,03	0,03	0,40	-	-	-	59-62
S30V	1,45	14,00	2,00	4,00	-	-	-	-	-	-	-	-	58-61
S35VN***	1,40	14,00	2,00	3,00	-	-	-	-	-	-	-	-	58-61
S60V (=CPM-440V)	2,15	17,00	0,40	5,50	0,40	-	-	-	0,40	-	-	-	56-58
S90V (=CPM-420V)	2,30	14,00	1,00	9,00	-	-	-	-	-	-	-	-	56-58
S110V**	2,80	15,25	2,25	9,00	-	-	-	-	-	-	2,50	-	58-61
Vanadis 4 Extra	1,40	4,70	3,50	3,70	0,40	-	-	-	-	-	-	-	60-65
ZDP-189	3,00	20,00	-	-	-	-	-	-	-	-	-	-	57-62